88
A Journal Of Contemporary American Poetry

Issue 1 - December 2001

Hollyridge Press
Venice, California

Managing Editor
Denise L. Stevens

Contributing Editors
Ian Randall Wilson
Eve Wood

© 2001 Hollyridge Press

All rights reserved under International and Pan-American Copyright Conventions. Published in the United States by Hollyridge Press.

Hollyridge Press
P.O. Box 2872
Venice, California 90294

Cover Design by D.L. Stevens

Manufactured in the United States of America by Lightning Source

ISBN: 0-9676003-4-0

88: A Journal of Contemporary American Poetry is published annually by Hollyridge Press. Please see the last pages of the volume for specific submission information. Copyright reverts to authors on publication though in the event of a reprint we ask for courtesy credit.

88's naming is something of a mystery. Some say it was named in homage to Alfred Stieglitz's *291*. Others suggest that the numerals are taken from the address of one of the editors' late relatives. Still another version is that the upright double-infinity signs suggest boundless imagination. It just may be that the anapest sounds good to the ear, feels good to the mouth.

Hollyridge Press is a small press publisher located in Venice, California. Using Print-On-Demand technology, Hollyridge Press, publishes primarily literary fiction. Print-On-Demand allows Hollyridge Press to maintain modest overhead through low initial print costs and minimal inventory. Books are always in print and available through wholesaler Ingram.

Contents

Ronald Alexander
    In Repose 1

Jack Anderson
    Boats On The Water 2

Marcia Arrieta
    Vulnerable To The Outside World 3
    The Poet 4

Barry Ballard
    Journey 5
    Visit Of Light 6

Amiri Baraka
    Every Full Moon 7
    Yeh? 8
    Actual Off 9

Bruce Beasley
    Preface 10
    Hazard 12
    Origin 13

Molly Bendall
    Civilized 14
    Holiday 15

Rick Bursky
    The Talion 16

Justin Israel Cain
    How The Fair Grappler Fed The Fishes 17

Tom Chandler
    To The Woman At The Red Edge Motel 18

Tricia Cherin
    Laundry 19

Nels Goñi Christianson
    Late February 20

Ann Colburn
    Confessional 22

Wanda Coleman
    Darwinian Ebb 23
    Revisiting Fear And Memphis 24

Patricia Corbus
    Cafe Politico 25
Mary Crow
    Frontiers 26
Daria Donovan
    Gathering At The Ark 28
Annie Finch
    Belly 30
Stewart Florsheim
    Thirst 31
Chris Forhan
    Where The Past Went 32
Richard P. Gabriel
    Good Evening, Bitter 33
    Unnormalized Models 34
Louis Gallo
    Letter To My Sister 35
Richard Garcia
    Odds Against Tomorrow 37
Shirley Graham
    The Butterfly Man 38
    Guernica 39
    A Conversation Overheard. 41
Julie Grass
    Beyond Splendor 44
William Greenway
    The University Of Hell 46
Susan Hahn
    Petit Point II 47
    Petit Point III 48
Matt Hart
    Over A Wide Field Of Thought 49
    In Human Resonance 50
    Monster 51
Kristen Havens
    In Juarez 52

George Higgins
    Villanelle 56
    For Billy Higgins 57
Tony Hoagland
    Procedure 58
    Illness And Its Metaphors 60
    Summer Night 62
Christina K. Hutchins
    Between Here And There 63
Mark Irwin
    Heart 66
Roy Jacobstein
    Writer's Block 67
Kate Knapp Johnson
    Wheelchair Pirouette 68
    Everything Alive 69
Karen Kevorkian
    Hunger 71
Susan Kolodny
    Psychiatry's Wife 74
Richard Kostelanetz
    Recircuits 76
Peter Levitt
    Essay: Everything Is Permitted In The Imagination ... 77
Gary Lilley
    Prayer To Saint James Byrd Of Jasper, Texas 82
Gerald Locklin
    William Klein 83
    Young Chet 84
Jeffrey McDaniel
    The Mirror In Which I Will Be Judged 87
Fred Moramarco
    Spots Of Time 89
Christopher Moylan
    The Hill 90
Elisabeth Murawski
    Glass 92

Muriel Nelson
    Gargoyle's Ankyloglossia 93
D. Nurkse
    Driving West With Ragnar Nurkse 94
    The Formal Gardens At Xaia 95
    A Song Of Pacification 96
Louis Phillips
    Johnny Inkslinger Journeys Out To The Bronx. 97
James Reiss
    Moosehead Lake 98
Lee Rossi
    Dust 100
Amanda Schaffer
    Inebriology 102
Barry Silesky
    Medicine 103
Anne Silver
    Goal 104
    Uncle! 106
Rick Smith
    [Attach Cable. . .] 108
    Pebble Game 109
Adrienne Su
    Early Work 111
    Modernization 112
Virgil Suárez
    Tracks 113
Elaine Terranova
    Day And Night 115
    The First Time 116
David Trinidad
    Coda To The 'Stuck In The Car' Scene 118
William Trowbridge
    Coach Said 122
Lee Upton
    Roman Baths 123

Amy Uyematsu
    These Upheld Arms 124
    Sukoshi / Little Bites 125

David Wagoner
    On Being Asked To Discuss Poetic Theory 127
    In The Fog 128
    Good Night 129

Jesse Waters
    A New Walk 130

Charles Harper Webb
    Purple Cow 131
    Being Charles H. Webb, Ph.D. 132

Roger Weingarten
    Into The Mouth Of The Rat 133

Kathleene K. West
    'End The Heartbreak And Embarrassment . . .' 140

Eve Wood
    Review: *God* by Debora Gregor 142

Gail Wronsky
    De Grotesco 143
    De Criminal 144
    De Muse 145

Dean Young
    Redux Telemachus 146
    Prayer To A Window 148
    Embryoyo 150

Contributors
Guidelines

Ronald Alexander

IN REPOSE

It's an Indian summer night and he doesn't want to run the air. We surrender to the heat, extinguish the lights, pile our clothes on the carpet. We're entwined in our shorts on the living room floor, watching an Italian film; I sit close to the open window, propped against the sofa, and he's stretched out on his back with his head on my lap. The film proves hard to follow: subtitles compress at the bottom of the screen; key words are lost in the translation. Still, we understand everything. And I'm not really focused on the movie: it's enough to listen to the squeaky violin on the soundtrack and look down through the inconstant light at his face. His eyes are closed, his lips parted. His left hand rests on his stomach; his right is draped across my shins. I watch the movement of his chest as he breathes, taking this opportunity to study his body in repose. The flickering light transforms him: a bas relief in blue and yellow and green until a shift on screen floods his body with crimson, accentuating the effects of an afternoon in the sun and revealing the patina of mist on his skin. There's roundness to his physique: the muscles curve into one another—there's spirit in his form. His neck, his shoulders, his chest, his stomach, his legs: I can't discriminate. I can't ignore his wrists because they're attached to his legs and I can't remember his feet because I'm looking at his knees. His boxers fit loosely at the waist, the white cotton clings, and for a moment I consider arousing him, before deciding that the only proper thing to do is to let him sleep to escape this heat.

Jack Anderson

BOATS ON THE WATER

Night comes cooler and earlier these nights
And people go sooner
Up from their tables out on the lawn
Into the cottages lining the lake.
Screen doors keep shutting. Yet some people stay
Clearing the tables, scraping the plates
With their bits of salads, Jell-O moulds, cakes.
Then the lawns are empty. Porch lights flicker off.
But here and there windows are beacons of warmth.
Inside, perhaps,
A mother is telling a sleepy child
An old legend she made up this very moment
About an Indian princess who once lived here
Who was sweet and kind and helped little animals;
Or everyone reads encircled by hush
Before going to bed wrapped up in the darkness,
Letting silence deepen. The silence grows deeper.
Yet even this late there comes the sound,
The creak and plash,
Of boats moving somewhere out on the water:
Not boats we think are moving toward us,
Not boats we may know,
Just boats on the water late at night moving,
Moving long ago and moving still now.

Marcia Arrieta

VULNERABLE TO THE OUTSIDE WORLD

1

she could not measure the distance between
window and tree

her hands froze
like a clock caught in ancient irish bells

2

she did not know when everyone had stopped listening
she no longer spoke

her bed became coastline entering sea calm
she could not walk the cliffs

birds began to visit: kestrels, a green woodpecker,
occasionally merlins   feathers fell in front of her eyes

3

she saw the figurehead of a lion
removed from the wreck

and could not remember
when they all had left her

alone on the peninsula
monastic stone   wild grass

Marcia Arrieta

THE POET

to be stripped
as easily as air

a human body
suspended

hills   fields
compelling

the head
elsewhere

Barry Ballard

JOURNEY

I think it's less of "going there" and more
of being "pulled" through my study door, down
through the passages of the books that line
my walls, down through the center of my desk,
down through the earth's crust to that milky core
where its thought is stirred and settled, down
through its tentative orbit in which I'm
already susceptible to the death

of its collapse, down through its spark of history
and explosion (that wed duality
of "matter" and "thought") where at last I am
the question behind it and the would-be
fullness or void of whatever it is
that I wish I could grasp in my own two hands.

Barry Ballard

VISIT OF LIGHT

There's something shimmering in the river
that doesn't belong to the river or
to me. It's something temporal that pours
itself over the surface in a quiver
of light, skimming the quiet boil and roll
of water through the canyons of limestone
and live oak trees. And when kneeling alone
at the edge of its body (swallowed whole

in the luminous drift), I can almost
feel the cooled remnants of last night's starlight
exchanging elements in the descending
layers of falloff, exposing the ghost-
like outline of each constellation to life
and its unwinding, its stall, its bending.

Amiri Baraka

EVERY FULL MOON

    I get horrible letters
    From Ghosts

Demanding
Money

        I pay them
Because there are no laws
Against *Instortion*
The legal term for "Threatening
Demands for Money, &c
Made by Dead People."

    But if you burn
These "Willliams"
 's what the Ghosts
call 'em,)

    & say the same words
Mantan Moreland
Used to,
      when he was
          pulling Security
For Charlie Chan's
        "Number One Son"

"Oh Oh!"
        "Oh Oh!"
                "Oh Oh!"
<u>THREE</u> <u>TIMES</u>!

        The Ghosts might not stop sending then letters
           Right Away

        But they probably wont be able
           to Find Out
                Where you went to!

Amiri Baraka

We heard Monk

Had met

The Devil

Next time we see Monk,

We ask him, "What was the Devil

Like?"

Monk say,

"He wa'dn't callin himself

The Devil

When he hit on me.

Amiri Baraka

✿o ACTUAL OFF

I asked
>   A WOODEN NEGRO
>   WAS HE
>   LAUGHING
>   OR
>   CRYING

"I don't know",
>   he sd,
>   >   "Tell me
>   >   >   The difference"?

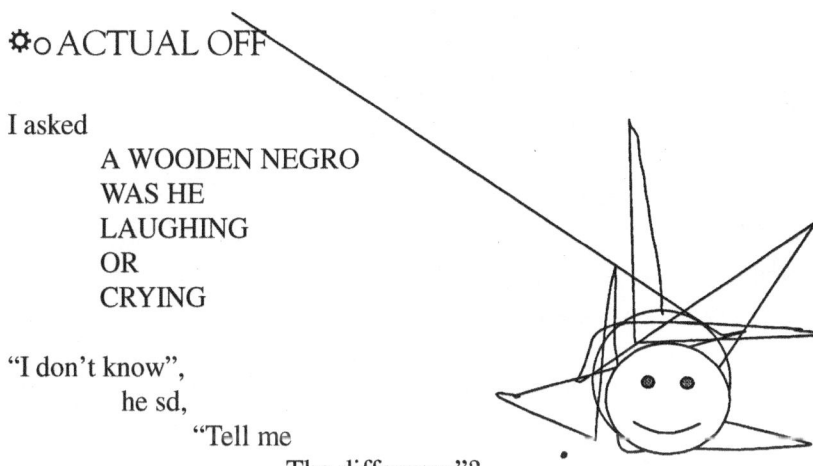

Bruce Beasley

PREFACE

But the final lexicon, my lexicon says,
exists only in the mind of God—

Then open the bound

red leather of this Fallen
provisional dictionary

& enter its chambers with praise,

dice-choice
Jubilate:
its temporal labels,
syllabification dots & secondary variables,
its subsense
numbers.

Its virgules / *small rods*
my rod & shaft
(rod wherewith thou smitest/rod that comforts me)

Lexical
journeywork: morphology,
shape of the word. Made
flesh, & dwelt among us.

The turned
cube of each definition, recombinant
as dice: verb,
reverberant. Re-

verse: turn
back. *The final lexicon,*

my lexicon says,
exists only in the mind of God. The pilgrim's

daybook, passages
unbooked, arrival times
unschedulable,

destination
determined only at the port of disembarking.

Bruce Beasley

HAZARD

What's
hazarded here, what lots
cast for the shucked
clothes? The die,
haphazard, clashes
its mate, & settles.
Settles it all, chance
by chance.

Con-
tingent: to touch
together.

This salvage
operation,

dredging the accidental.

Savage operation.

Who wears
the won garments
now, split
seams, their ill
fit?

Bruce Beasley

ORIGIN

So the origin

of *puzzle* remains unknown,
itself riddled, insoluble.
Just over *Pyracantha*, fire-thorn. Origin

as a rising-up: In the beginning out
of nothing what
arose. Incipience

as ascension: fire-thorn's
signal-smoke, etymology
unpuzzling its originary

trace. So here, among
the warped, rain-sodden jigsaw-pieces, go
ahead—you know you want to—

release again the dice from your restless grip. . .

Molly Bendall

CIVILIZED

Who was that artist again? What's his
name? I'll look it up

in my library of bark, my bookcase of mud and bricks.
This little hut bulges like a growth. Storms cheat

and snicker. That ridge, it could, it *could* be the Riviera.
                       There's plenty of water and plenty

to want. Unfortunately, I have only one mirror

so I can't see how my hair looks in back. I wake up
and before my eyes open

I swear my piano is sitting there glistening,

                all its seeds in place.

Molly Bendall

HOLIDAY

    Banishment and exile scent

the water, so I'm wading in a big aperitif.
        It moved me, love-drop, when you
allowed me to help you. The beast was

    quite tame with its little chickory bangs.

Wasn't it a shame I kept thinking of someone else?

You rescued me
too. "Come to my getaway at the shore."

  We threw clothes, appliances in—
pitch it in, smoke it up—

    the ocean's a wince away.
        Couldn't we have summered?

Twice jumbled and still I crack the rain
        wide open.

Rick Bursky

THE TALION

There was a burning in my chest as I returned to work
after lunch, reminding me of a sharper pain
I felt between my shoulder blades a few moments earlier.
Glancing at my reflection in a store window
I saw an arrow stretched from my back
as if it were a line directing the world to my pain.
Could this be the result of confusion in the delicatessen
when a woman became angry because I was served first?
I spent the rest of the afternoon standing in my office,
afraid a chair might force the arrow deeper.
The door remained closed, not for fear the author
of my punishment would return, but to avoid the questions.
Everyone deserves something; a life unpunished is a life unexamined.
I once bet a cousin I could peel an orange
without breaking the continuous curl of thick skin.
If I succeeded the orange would be mine,
otherwise my new coat would be his.
The week of practice was never mentioned.
Is this the confession that explains my tragedy?
Or was it because I watched the unfaithful
smoke of religion smudge the wall of an orthodox church
and prayed for selfish indulgence? Could you explain
an arrow between your shoulder blades?
Blood stained my underclothes as I rode the bus home;
a red trail of footprints to my door. The shaft removed,
a growth of dark flesh is the reminder. Before a heavy rain
it ripples with pain like a pebble dropped in water, a warning
to close windows and bring in laundry before leaving for work.

Justin Israel Cain

HOW THE FAIR GRAPPLER
FED THE FISHES

The master winks like I'm a hot co-ed
in a haiku swimsuit, but I'm just an ignoramus
wine boy at Trimalchio's feast
preparing for the lunch bell. That's when
the guests will cry for more
Greco-Roman olive oil and I'll try
my legal death grips!

This is the part where the fugitive
gains passage on a spice boat
and nearly makes it to Macedonia,
but the Captain's drunk
and sails into some rocks.
The boat sinks and everyone dies.

That about covers it.

Tom Chandler

TO THE WOMAN AT THE RED EDGE MOTEL

Some tourist of love
in his cheap suit of longing
will elbow the bar
in the lounge of no last names,
dip his cuff accidentally
in your seven & seven
and ask you to dance
to the faint moan of muzak,
perfume your earrings
with breath mints and gin
as the lights grow yet dimmer
and his hand on the switch
hovers inches away
from the slick red edge
of your hungover heart
with its faded no vacancy sign.

Tricia Cherin

LAUNDRY

Our species used to gather at the river
and pound raiment
hide and weaving
on rocks

This was inconvenient surely
when the weather was inclement
but with dear company
and the rightness of sky
I envy
that BUZZ of familial industry
the matrimony of purpose to place

Now we go to laundry rooms
with electric lights and spin cycles
simulacra of the amps and decibels
of sky and river
sodden clothes in wire baskets
imitatio of feathers in bowls of rock

Nels Goñi Christianson

LATE FEBRUARY

I work in the garden as it begins to rain
I wear no hat, am almost bald
the sky and weather come down
slowly at first
so I prune roses old and new
Rubaiyat, Nicole, Elizabeth Taylor
Moonstone
imagining the places where names are born
and how a small plant growing
can become a world to a child
and a man
the rain falls thicker
my bulky sweat clothes keep me warm
somehow their wet exterior
makes a dry defense
and I continue with shears in hand
considering the Buddleia
which grew too large last season
and the guava that tenders branches
in toward the tree
I do not move quickly
or count the raindrops on my forehead
or those running down my cheeks
I survey the garden
the fig tree is bare and wide
last year its boughs bent to the ground
I want to raise them back
so I cut the lower stems

I move steadily and in each move
remember the pink and purple larkspur
that grew under another fig
wet with another rain
when my only concern was climbing

Ann Colburn

CONFESSIONAL

ah, love, it is your body I miss
your palm cupping my breast
your eyes which will not relinquish me

loss gives no warning
even through long illness
when it is anticipated

unanticipated
its bite is merciless

no search and rescue
reaches this heart's core
lungs need time to remember
how deep breaths
can unfold my belly
from the points along my spine

I am talking of the physical here
simply the empty space

grief tricks me into belief
I see you coming through the garden
your intent clear

your scent unmistakable even in
a t-shirt fresh from the wash

yet this deeper yearning
is not the body's
it only carries the weight
manifest in tears

outside our window
pine needles still gleam with sun
against the bluest sky

Wanda Coleman

DARWINIAN EBB

what was there to begin with

nature in the foreground / unseen things sensed
resistance, therefore, without doubt
a scene where demonstrable horror is linked
to a minimum of means, the glimpse of a shadow
something seen but unrecognizable
in its imposing intimacy

out beyond Orion or encased at the onionlike core
of the self examining itself

one existing without the other yet in perfect if immaterial
correlation / lyricism unleashed and fragmentary
spotting the skin psyche / a form dissolving as it travels
room to room, breast to breast

vision recreating vision—the shapelessness of change
metamorphosis comes
reaching toward the whole imagined
a broken entirety.

how much of the future is missing?

whose past is found in that simple black stone on the sand?

seeing with the heart keeps
form out of character, preserves
the image in the light—divides
this moment from that ancient wholeness

in which we were captured in the margins
and breathed one breath

Wanda Coleman

REVISITING FEAR AND MEMPHIS

we gather in that place that speaks the having been
of civil war of uncivil assassination

sons named Oseola, daughters named Sojourner

marble monuments gleaned at twilight cast shade
across cold land, river to river, woman, child and man
dedicated to the memory of the murdered
damnable history exhumed by candlelight
etched on the scroll of martyrdom, the names of the butchered,
the diseased, the lynched and the starved—perished
in the name of race arrogance that they may ascend to those
heavenly lanes lined with Magnolias and stars
no longer the dreamers but The Dream recalled
on holidays when births are celebrated, and the justice
not yet received summoned sorely by weary-lipped prayer

whosoever put their blood in this soil, raise thy standard

Patricia Corbus

CAFE POLITICO

Here we talk only about ideas, those whores
Any stagehand can make any color by fooling
With cellophane, but they are even less, nothing
But clothes: khaki shirts, crotchless panties,

Simple white gowns, hot pants, black ties.
What loomed small and deadly in the camouflage
Of ringlets and mustaches?—Where are the epaulets,
The uniforms of the hussars, the satin negligees,

Stalin's trousers, your grandmother's bombazines,
And can our bodies be any different, dissolving
Into the ground as they do, while we talk and talk,
Gasping for air through layers of corduroy and lace?

Summer gone by, summer blooming—but O, friend,
I am tired. Even that gibbous moon is just a Dali
Moon, redly drooping over trees—a dinosaur moon,
Romantic and primitive, made for daily melting.

Mary Crow

FRONTIERS

I.
And still she climbed
through the gray land and gray leaves
filled with a murmur
like words. Two paths:
Between roots of olive trees
and that immense gray
that was sky as well as hills.

In a field across from her
a dozen tiny deer
grazed, animals
that she knew once spoke
Hebrew, before Babel, before the flood.

II.
Coming, as she did, to feel
like a cavewoman near
the entrance, she could see
how dark it was, how
stuffy, as she tried to push
the black. She bruised herself
against it. A wedge of light
brightened beyond.

III.
Could she be happy here?
Ivy smothered the castle.
In the mirror with rosettes at each corner
she caught his eye

above the crowd's shoulders,
and already she was
inserting words, a biography,
strolls in the park,
already—

IV.
She can imagine her twin
lost in the vastness of Prague
and at the door of the empty
office: wreckage of bookshelves
and papers, the you-ravine.

A crackle in the air and also
balminess in which she pauses
to note the bark's silver,
forsythia's yellow, the forbidden's
electric flow.

Daria Donovan

GATHERING AT THE ARK

she holds
in her cat claw

an old rumble
steaming off the path
and into her bear nostrils

a signal
that there are others coming

a reassuring bellow
through the trees

an answer
howling from a rocky ledge

snake skin
loosened by the ground

eyes shut
quickly open

appears the she-moon
as a new litter of tears

a dreamy den
warmed by mothers
wintering with heavy breath

as a womb
nursing now
at a different fire

her place
certain
in the benevolent scheme

and so
bear sets down
the snake

and doe stands unafraid
with cat

timid heartbeat
rustling near

ah, at last
the hare
has found her way

Annie Finch

BELLY

My belly thickens like a stem,

my belly is tethered by your days.

My body turns in place of clouds,

I grow like a pane of open glass.

My breasts go heavy to meet you here.

Stewart Florsheim

THIRST

My mother and I are given careful instructions
on how to hasten her death.
Once you stop drinking, it's only a matter of days.
When I was a boy, I was so frail
I could barely walk up a flight of stairs.
Dr. Turnauer told my mother to force me to eat:
Try anything. Raw egg yolks in chocolate milk.
I can still see my mother separating the yolk
from the egg white until she only had the yellow center
back in its cracked shell,
the albumen dripping reluctantly into the porcelain sink.
She would drop the yolk into the dark brown liquid
and beat it as hard as she could,
then hold up the container to see if the yolk had disappeared
but it was elusive, the light always detecting
the yellowish wisps that would help me survive.

Chris Forhan

WHERE THE PAST WENT

Farewell, fedoras for the men, farewell, furs for the ladies,
they're flung in a trunk, the trunk
flung in the room of what's long gone:
rumble seats, saddle shoes, slide rules, whiff of a rose
plucked in some forgotten summer, so long,
so long to the popular song on the old Victrola,
to scraps of the past swept into shadows,

trapped in a musty room, door overgrown with ivy
and rusted shut, the busted Underwood is there
with its missing *o*, books on Burmese cooking, spines cracked,
        chattering
Teletypes, rattling teeth of a dead sand dollar, tortoiseshell
comb, tin box of ribbon and string, the light as it looked
that day the sun went red before an August rain,
it's all there, it hasn't gone, it's not coming back,

dirt under Dad's nails, Dad in the dirt,
dust spun into the air by a truck you watched,
through tears, disappear up a hill,
you were six years old, now you're five,
you stretch your arms before you—in one fist
the licorice bought with a nickel you earned
by being good, and in the other, the nickel, not yet spent.

Richard P. Gabriel

GOOD EVENING, BITTER

The evening is cracked
by understandings and slivers
of lights beneath doorways,
a broken bowl the color of glass
roses still rocks, and the cup
emptied of tea still holds
its folded lemon among sifted
leaves.

Beneath your shut bedroom door
the crack of light is darkened
by your passing.

I wait in its shadow.

Richard P. Gabriel

UNNORMALIZED MODELS

This is the recipe for this.
Random fields,
exponential models,
motivated from (turn

your head
and say natural language
processing

). Segmenting and
labeling sequences. A
framework

       based on
conditional random fields
offering several

advantages over
hidden Markov models and
stochastic grammar.

(she was thin
I thought
not normal I
liked her segments
enough to fill
the universe with a 2-d
string)

Second, we derive an equivalence
between the well-known
technique of boosting and maximum
likelihood for exponential
models. The idea of
unnormalized models plays
a key role.

Louis Gallo

LETTER TO MY SISTER

Dear Ruth,
the hibiscus I planted last May
once exploded in sultry, carmine glory.
Three, four new flowers every day.
Now, December, it has shriveled
to a black, withered stalk
rising feebly from the ice,
the remnant of some minor evil.
The skunks have returned,
an entire tribe of nervous rodents
squealing madly at midnight,
thumping against the joists
in the crawl space under our house.
I sprayed Lysol down the vent
to scare them away. They don't scare.
I imagined them rising like ghosts
through floorboards, exuding foul gas
to paralyze us all on the spot.
So when you called I was prepared.
You're hungry, you said, always hungry,
never satisfied, ravenous, empty.
Everything is broken,
the kids tinker with your mind,
Mom maxes Visa out of loneliness,
the new car sputters, lurches on I-10,
life gets harder each day and heavy
like a teaspoon of neutron star.
Of course I agree.
We dipped to forty-three below
with the wind chill,
and the dew point read negative.
I live in a place where washrags

dehydrate overnight into stiff swatches
like American flags on the moon.
Skunks!
The shy little Nissan had to be towed
one hundred miles in a blizzard.
Then that Hitlerian virus sacked us,
and Claire reacted to her antibiotic—
red welts erupting on her puny body;
I delved into chasms of paranoia
and rang the doctor after midnight
to beg for a smidgen of hope.
Christmas was jolly. We all had fever.
So you're right:
our children should love us more,
massage our feet, offer sacrifices.
Clutches should not burn up.
Mom should split Visa with a scissors.
But I have exactly 37 Visa's myself.
How could I thrive without them?
The purple splotch on my arm
has deepened into a fissure.
We're exhausted, dread birthdays,
eye obituaries with relief,
check for occult blood.
Yet not long ago
my hibiscus flared with beauty;
I inspected it every day,
admired and feasted upon it,
once burying my face in the womb
of its leafy flesh.
I think ice has not killed it.
I think those wondrous red wings
rooted in wet blue-black earth
will return one day.
So how can I not be tempted
to sing as we grieve?

Richard Garcia

ODDS AGAINST TOMORROW

A man always dreams about what he wants or what
he's afraid of. I was really wailing on my sax
at the Blackhawk—the music dangling, twirling
slowly in a spiral like a mobile made of black
and white rectangles when the cash register chimed in
right on key with my solo, and everything
went silent: reflections off glasses, the blue light
over the mirror, red glow of cigarettes—everything
became a dim flickering of crab claws in silty water.
Once I jumped off a window ledge,
after a lifetime, it seemed, of searching for this girl.
Not my type really. Thin, the kind of girl, if you didn't like,
you'd call mousy. No tits. Tomboy, too. Anyway,
I gave up looking for her, and just as I was leaning
into tomorrow too far to go back, I saw a door open,
she walked in and I knew she was looking for me.
I woke with this sadness in my stomach, something
without a cure, a crazy longing to get back in the past
and stay there. I wondered, if I threw myself out a window,
would I see her again? Sometimes I pace my room, smoking,
the lights off, thinking of maybe calling my ex-wife, Kitty.
She always said I'd end up in a room like this: bathroom
down the hall, hot plate, a sink I piss in. I'm pacing, smoking,
listening over and over to Monk's "Misterioso." The notes
slightly off balance, hesitant, excited, like a man climbing up
and down a ladder in the dark. I pace around my room step
by step until I hear the silver slash of Art Blakey's drumroll—
that's my cue to stop, turn, and pace again in the opposite direction.

Shirley Graham

THE BUTTERFLY MAN

How like the butterfly man, pinned to the wall by an evening breeze. Blown off-course by every passing car's tailwind. Poor creature. Poor man. And it's not as though he's all fragility. His man's body is a Greek statue: Zeus in his shoulder muscles, sleek Achilles around the thighs. On calm days, he has the strength of four men and enough beauty for five. But any degree of assertive weather brings out the vulnerability in his wings. Translucent patches of icy color held together by a network of nerves, the wings are a walking, moving painting—but painful, painfully sensitive. Wind hurts them, rain hurts them; to have them bumped into is torture. So the butterfly man keeps his distance from people and things to avoid being jarred. Again, poor man. It should be enough burden that he's unlike the rest. Nature might have compensated by giving him flight, but that solace is also nearly denied. For now, the wings are pure decoration—beauty and liability. There is a small hope that, if he lives long enough, his muscle-heavy man's body will age and shrivel so that just before death the wings will be able to lift and support his diminishing body and he'll fly.

Does he live for that day? It would be a bitter joy to keep as the sole source of hope. Perhaps he survives on the admiration of crowds. Maybe it is enough for him to have loved once, to have folded his wings over the arching back of a grateful, sensitive woman, if that has happened—and one may doubt. Then again, the wings might be good company for him. Maybe they sing to each other, color to color, nerve to nerve.

Shirley Graham

GUERNICA

—After Picasso

A woman screams, My child!
Inside the city,
inside the house of the city.

Hold the light up to it.
See the boy's broken head
dangling over his mother's lap, her own
neck thrown back in unnatural terror as
she kisses the bull of Spain,
bull whose severed head still floats
near its body, snorting, raging.

Because someone wanted something.
Let the light stay on in the house of the city
that all may see how someone
wanted something.

The noble horse's legs scatter under him.
Everywhere he steps he tramples head, arms, torso
torn away from the hero who would have ridden him,
the hero dead and clutching pieces of sword.
A woman screams, hold the lamp up to it!

Even the birds are torn from the sky.

Another woman kneels in the light of the destruction,
her breasts electrified by grief, her mouth
a gasping scream.

The house of the city is blue with spilled blood,
even its roof is torn away,
torn and fallen on the people it should protect,
the people of the house of the city,
the blue people, the screaming people,
the dead people.

Hold the light up while you can.
See what someone wanted. This is not
weather, the bombs coming through the window
with the breeze, the jagged,
the murderous points. This is design
and desire, the blue blood
of woman, man, mad horse and fuming bull,
the single funeral flower, bombs
at the window, torn bodies,
the fallen house.

Let the light stay on that all may see
what someone wanted.

Shirley Graham

A CONVERSATION OVERHEARD BETWEEN ROBERT WALSER AND A VISITOR AT THE HERISAU ASYLUM

OR, NO, NOT A CONVERSATION, A MONOLOGUE, YES, YES, THAT'S IT, A VERITABLE SPEECH

No, believe me, sir, I am entirely happy here. What more could I desire than this pleasant little life, I ask you? My daily walks are mine entirely to perform. I need not cede the performance of them to anyone else at all. Not even the fact that no one else would take them if I tried to give them away, not even that small fact can prevent me from being entirely satisfied, or I should say ecstatic, with the truth of my having these walks all to myself. And as you can see, who so graciously share today's with me, they are indeed splendid walks. Astounding walks. Heavenly walks. Here, under the trees of the park, this park of life, if I may be allowed to wax rhapsodic.

Which reminds me, park is precisely the symbolic essence of my existence here. I live as in a park. Just like the child who comes with pocket money for ice cream and time enough for an entire day under the shade of the sycamore trees in the town's park and who spends that day running between the glint of bright climbing apparatus and cool damp pockets of newly mowed lawn, just like that am I pampered and delighted on every turn by the members of this splendid establishment. I am fed, bathed, discussed, examined, and made to lie down in green pastures. I am regularly awoken, aroused, assisted, addled, aerated and abated. In short, I am entirely cared for. Not content with merely administering personal alimentation and hygiene routines, my dear caretakers (although I hesitate to use such a clinical word for these people, these folk, this tribe, who are, in a word, family) even take pains to organize my free time by giving me the most delightful little tasks, little exercises, little games with which to busy my little head. Yesterday afternoon, for example, I had the pleasure to shell and sort the green peas which were to be served for dinner. Now, I can hear your protest before it is out of your mouth, and let me stop it there in mid air between your nose and mine. Yes, yes, I can hear you say, "But Walser, my good man, shelling peas is servant's stuff, no fitting activity for a literary man (I do not use the word genius, mind you, mark my newly acquired modesty) like yourself." But here, my dear friend, I must tell you that you are essentially and inessentially wrong. Shelling and sorting peas, what better way to spend an afternoon? Let all the heads of state gather in the universal kitchen to sort peas, and see how congenial men can become. Each tiny green orb, full of variation and shading, thoroughly individual in color and character, is a world to me. I give them names: Karina the angel pea, Malvio the green demon, Heinrich the serviceable, Sultan the squashed. And the pea shells, the green caves from which my population springs, fit so satisfyingly in the palm of the hand that only the joy of adding them to the beautiful pile below one's feet is sufficient incentive to let them go.

Now, my good Sir, you must begin to see the rich flavor of my days here in the park. I feel I have risen considerably in life station when I can call shelling peas and strolling a full day's work. And at night, I rest my walk-weary body, stretching it out the length of my cot, and fall dizzily, happily, giddily asleep to the gentle music of my neighbor's howls as stars of a sort dance and fidget gently overhead.

It's no wonder, when you stop to examine the rococo details of my life in this manner, that I no longer feel compelled to scramble with pen and paper to w-r-i-t-e, to communicate. Communication happens with every gesture in this place. I am known, fully known, as Walser the resident, the sheller of peas, the insatiable walker. I am met at every turn with recognition and understanding (I need not say, for the first time in my life). In short, I belong.

Now, while I am expounding in such a frank and expansive manner to you, who know me from another setting, I will admit that only on my walks, alone, do I feel fully myself, fully tuned to the environs. And only then does the welcome monologue begin, that familiar and eloquent drone, the narration of my existence. Yes, it is when my mind has the solitude and motion it needs to begin discussing with itself every aspect of the passing cowherd's boots, the road's mud puddles, and the leaves' many greens, it is then that I stretch my legs into a comfortable but productive amble, and thrive. Sometimes I dream of walking into my own narration, the scene I step onto blooming to the words I describe. To walk into my own words, what a delicious notion. There would be a walk which would never end.

But then again, it is also lovely, equally fine, to return from the evening walks to this fine facility, my private pea pod, and nestle myself in for the night. Dear friend, now that you see how very smug, how very green my life is here, I am sure you will never again wish me another.

Julie Grass

BEYOND SPLENDOR

On Easter mother wraps herself in fuzz
wears pastels and
strings of jelly beans
round her neck, ankles and wrists
eye pencils whiskers across her cheeks
and glue guns a white ball of feathers
on the seat of her pants.
She eats only carrots and lettuce
astroturfs the den
hopping from sofa to chair
twitching her nose.
I wear my pink leotard
and nestle close while mother
watches Harvey
and Bugs Bunny reruns.

July 4th is bolder
her hair corn-rowed into a centennial
of braids, each one clamped
with a red white or blue barrette,
she wakes me to John Phillip Sousa
dressed in a muumuu of stars and stripes,
serves me warm apple pie
and ice cream straight from the carton.
We are Suffragettes, Feminists, American women
marching through the living room
with placards of freedom and equality
lighting sparklers at dusk,
we 2 statues of liberty
weary beacons
in the night.

Her glee is raucous,
a wild all-consuming hilarity
that mushrooms and spreads
and robs me of the simple,
so that my threshold for joy is so high
I can't reach it
even with amphetamines and stilts.

William Greenway

THE UNIVERSITY OF HELL

It's open admissions, free tuition, A's for everyone,
but attendance is mandatory, and the classes seem eternal.
The pitchforks of the teaching assistants say no falling
asleep, no rest for the wicked, no soft answers
turning away wrath. They advance through the lower levels,
the core curriculum, each room packed and stifling—"Principles
of Envy" (prerequisite "Pride"), "Getting and Spending,"
"Advanced Rage." All old hat. The most popular courses
are "Escape Methods 101," and "History of Remorse."
Tired of the mill-stack smoke, the sinner-students try
to transfer—*Willing to Relocate*, they write,
but the flaming postman won't deliver, hands them
asbestos postcards: *If you're thinking of applying,
don't*. The restrooms are filthy, the graffiti
(*Satan Sucks*) never washed from the walls.
The elevators don't work—no one goes up anyway—
and *Not Smoking is Prohibited*

Everyone has tenure, even the students; they couldn't be fired
if they tried. The football program's well endowed, but except
when the Flies lose to the Angels once a millennium, the games
are intramural. There are no rules. The cheerleaders jump
and twitch and beat at their flaring skirts with blazing pompoms.
Howling the fight song "All Hope Abandon," the fans
in the stands in smoldering raccoon coats can hardly
see the players, silhouettes bashing each other
in the sulfurous light, trying to make the draft, though the big leagues
are full. Just as graduation is a cruel and empty ritual, the sopping
robes, the paper fans and programs catching fire, and then the walking
to applause across the stage to get that pre-signed, pre-approved
       entry form,
though all of them, even the *magma cum laude*, the Dishonor Students,
still have to stand in interminable lines, get the signature
of a smirking advisor, just to be freshmen all over again
because some people never learn.

Susan Hahn

PETIT POINT II

When the air is calm and on
clear nights with the wind so light,
dew drops form inside the hollows
of the grass between its joints
like kisses of small measure.
Certainly better than the deposit
which takes the shape of hoarfrost
or when the temperature falls low enough

to stitch flakes together into hex-
agonal patterns. When water molecules
conjoin, that violence
can sculpt a rigid lattice.
However beautiful and intricate

the fallen snow, if it survives the spring
and then the summer, it will
turn to ice and then to glacier.
And all avalanches of passion
will not bring even
a petit point of pleasure.

Susan Hahn

PETIT POINT III

When the days and nights were of equal length
and the autumn equinox warned
the birds to migrate toward the Equator
to escape the falling temperatures, we drove
up and down a single block—landlocked—
and watched the leaves in their last dance

of color. How flushed and fevered
they were in their final daze—
a petit point of terror, their panic
sewn into the strict canvas
of nature, the extreme stage

in the fear sequence before us.
The plummet toward earth crust
where all becomes organic litter—
the dream over—was days away.
Reel and keel. Past topsoil
and humus, the interlock
with silt and sand and fragments
called *parent material,*

came so fast, the zero
down to unweathered bedrock—
a place where you are now woven
into an indecipherable, invisible pattern.

Matt Hart

OVER A WIDE FIELD OF THOUGHT

Nicole says that as a child she repeatedly stuck
her fork in a socket. Now she can barely fly a sentence.
Everyday she asks, What does control me mean?
And when she arches her back I lose whatever
I was about to say. I end up slipping—Which is more
useful, to decry or to declaim? In every direction,

Milk does a body. . . The word of the day
is terror all night. The wheels go round on the busted
machine. It's all so hard on the bus driver
no matter who he happens to be. The soft soap skull
or the scoliosis hatter. But it goes beyond them to me,
the dreamsicle melting. I guess I know now
why not to trust the burner. Defeat in hand,

the concession stand shut down.
I see an Amy in waves. I see a Lara in rehab. Kate
smashed a mouse and tossed it into the dumpster.
She was so sorry, but the trap got it first. She only
put it out of its mystery.

Wrap me in newspaper,
float me out to sea. Give me coat hangers, or give me. . .
As I said, the word is barricade,
but there are also margins, projections, forecasts.
In a mechanical way, I spill my sandwich.
The exterminator mumbles

from the back of the room. If snap-traps won't do it we could
go with a spray, but the box-and-gnaw method has proven effective
in recent months. It's nearly Christmas. How much
is that bleeding in the window?

Matt Hart

IN HUMAN RESONANCE

Blistered in my blue suit
I wait for you (remembering a ball
of orange string). I love today

on purpose. It's almost noon, and I am
preparing to cut up my art books.
Toulouse Lautrec will drink the house down.
Paul Klee will be relieved on a wall

of wet children. Mike is over fixing
the furnace, and the house smells like burning
dust. To speak in code is to relax. Saturday
again. Hailstorm works. Quotes Coleridge best,
who lovest best. Thank you sad astronaut.

Thank you in advance professor Y. Waiting,
I answer an unglued subscriber: Dear Guy,
Sorry to inform you, we have folded our napkins
and put away the silver. The PO Box collapsed.
Do not hold your breath. We are deep
incommunicado. Your Forklift Connection,
Uncle Dispersion

      Probably this note will end up mistaken.
I have to have lunch: hot peppers and decaf.
Mike tells me the former is bad for my stomach.
The latter is hard on your liver. The first

is a paraphrase, the second a quote. Note
the falling off, the loss of intensity.
O monster, come back.

Matt Hart

MONSTER

A piece of work, smug and terrible.
In the Mood comes on the radio, distracts me
2 or 3 minutes, then I'm back to the thing as it is:
peppermint or a bolt. Eventually, we'll have to
assemble ourselves and stand up to

confetti. Right now though, I'm wondering
about surfaces, planes, sunfish on the bank, gasping.
Have I done this correctly or merely made a mess
with a hundred-pound bag of black sand?
Is anybody coming out to meet me?

A woodpecker in the backyard hammers
a mirror. Fall is falling fine. Anyway, I'm tired
and fed up with summer: fireworks, river-air,
men standing around smoking, saying
things I hear only consonant bits of. I'll tell you:

Box spring. Bull fight. Hiss. Just sounds.
My head out the window waiting for things to change.
Little kids smash bottles, torture lizards, burn
anything in the lot next to our house.
Trash goes out on Thursday. I rake

the first wrinkled specimens of leaves. When I feel
prepared I am nicer. What does paying attention mean?
Pass your paper to the person on your left.

Kristen Havens

IN JUAREZ

I. Morning

It is just another day in Juarez.
Las fresas make their way on the eight *peso* bus,
pale blue with fissured windows,
the seat backs tacked to the ceiling
and fastened with bear rope.

In between their toes is southern dust,
sweat mingling with the cologne
and last-minute dabs of holy water
given by *abuelita*.

Most are small town
with a secondary education
and a duffel packed with hand-made blouses.
All are searchingly urban,
black platforms and ankle tattoos
branded en route, in D.F.,
that city of smoke and palm trees.

Here, Juarez, is where the *las fresas* come
with scrubbed chins and fingers,
fast to fill the work bowl.

The bus swings a gentle curve
one yard from the U.S. border.
The doors pull apart and the pretty girls disembark, giggling,
knapsacks flashing past buildings with blackened windows,
party flyers and slanted advertisements ripped from the sides.

There is a sigh in the sidewalks
as they brush past the beggars, *tortas* shops,
rusted Coke machines
and puddles full of crushed drugs,
pills of varying shades settling into sediment.

The men flick matches and groan.
Las fresas. They have arrived.

II. Afternoon

The *maquiladoras* do things to you.
I know this, after nine months
among sewing machines,
bobbins and things spinning in place
while my blood thins,
and I become nothing but a servant.

In Puebla I babysat
for the children of doctors.
They paid me well and helped me
with my biology.
My mother was so proud.

Mirella, you have patrons, she would say.
Sí, but they have nothing to give me
but kind words and encouragement.
I need money for the university.

UNAM, in Coyoacan, is big with intellectuals,
murals creeping giant up its side.
Frida and Diego stalk around its periphery.
It is where I want to be.

When they saw me off they told me to be careful.
Do not work too hard. Save time for your studies.

It is more difficult than you think, though,
when you work in a factory.

Twelve hours a day you watch this bobbin spin,
feeling your back bones fold in upon each other
as your eyes dry and stick.
You try reading biology books all night.

Six months ago I quit the university.
Medical school is so expensive,
and the money I make is barely enough
to pay for Fridays at the club.

But I will go back, I know. After a rest.

III. Evening

It was not unexpected, when Mirella went missing.
Things like this happen daily in Juarez.
Las fresas hang heavy on this branch,
and almost beg for picking.

But still.

Alba, *su hermana*, came later,
to save for law school.
Unlike Mirella, she is not a dancer.
We watch her hard, squinting at her small tits.

Alba has an infant, so we know she's not innocent.

But she runs too fast for us,
straight home to the hut after dinner.
True, she is short and brown, but she would do
if she weren't such a bitch.

But Alba does not go out like the others.
She hoards her money well,
spending it on this strange campaign
she calls a protest.

Every weekend
she paints pink crosses on telephone poles.
This is for the federales, she says.
Someone must come to find my sister.

We toss bottle caps at her and laugh.
What are you doing, Alba, in your waterless shack?
She thinks we are aimless, because we don't work,
but that is not the case.

We labor, hard, on Friday nights,
when *las fresas* come at us clean and earringed,
their long legs stirring behind nylon.
Mira, Alba. Do you think we're useless now?

She always moves past us faster on Fridays.
And on Saturdays another cross goes up,
mixed paint in the windowless hut,
her baby inhaling the loose fumes.

George Higgins

VILLANELLE

(Spielberg visited an inner city school in response to a class of black students who had laughed inappropriately at a showing of his movie about the holocaust "Schindler's List.")

When Steven Spielberg spoke at Oakland High
A custodian swept up the shattered glass,
replaced the broken clocks to satisfy

the Governor, who was preoccupied
with becoming President, with covering his ass.
When Steven Spielberg spoke at Oakland High

the District found diminishing supplies
of disinfectant and toilet paper stashed
away, so they replaced the clocks instead to satisfy

the cameras and the press that they had rectified
the deficiencies among the underclass.
When Steven Spielberg spoke at Oakland High

the students didn't seem dissatisfied
about the cover up, just happy to be out of class.
The custodian replaced the broken clocks to satisfy

this need we have to falsify
the truth in subservience to cash.
When Steven Spielberg came to Oakland High
the custodian replaced the broken clocks.

George Higgins

FOR BILLY HIGGINS

After Philip Larkin

That cymbal you rake, sweeping and scuffing, calls
Like Pharaoh "I want you to go to the brushes,"
And in my eyes your hi-hat never stalls

Lifting up its pitch between the cadenced rush
Of cocktail glasses, chatter, and scattered anecdotes,
Your side men sitting down as though in prayer—

Yes, do that thing; please bend those notes!
While others dawdled, shifting in their chairs,
Last night I watched you sitting just off stage

Scatting the notes a week or two before you died.
I focused on your sallow face the program pages
Crumpled in your hands, the swelling. . . I tried

To concentrate, to listen, to summon up the voice
I wished my father had. My stand-in, my namesake
Creator, combining strokes with tenderness.

You conjured up the living breath, caressed
the sounds once more before the final take.

Tony Hoagland

PROCEDURE

That was an intimate moment
when the dental hygienist
snapped a latex glove on her slim hand
and entered my mouth with her steel instrument.

Picking the dead meat from between my teeth,
looking down into the hole of me,
it felt like we had moved rather quickly
                past the level of small talk,

down to where the cities of bacteria
are starting their civilizations
among the columns of dead bone

and the old discolored metal
gleams wetly in the dark.

When my mother was sick she was
speechless like this.
She made me drive her to another town
                to get her hair done
because she didn't want somebody she knew
operating on the top of her head,
combing her last earthly crop of hair
                over the lesions,
clucking their tongue in pity.

That's how I know it's unavoidable to be here
on my back in the reclining chair,
mouth open like a dead soldier
yielding up my dirty information,

because I'm just a cavity
of memory and tears

and I know this is a kind of practice,
a preparatory procedure
for that day in the future
when they are going to shine their light
into my darkest, most shameful crevice
                      and take me out of it.

That's when—
past charm and past complaint—
that's when we'll see
what the soul is made of.

Tony Hoagland

ILLNESS AND ITS METAPHORS

One day she said she would never again
as long as she lived remove her clothes
for one more fucking doctor.

Another time: "Why *not* lie
if it makes them feel like they are
doing me some good?"

*

Because it had been explained to us
that her body was a sort of battlefield,
when she took her medicine we saw
the good soldiers of the chemicals

riding into battle with the bad
army of the mutant cells—gunfire and smoke,
clash of flashing swords;
she was the ravaged earth beneath their hooves.

*

Later I would come to think of pain
as the way in which a person
is persuaded to get off the premises
of an expensive hotel,
after their stay is ended,

the unwanted guest refusing to leave,
hanging around the lobby, hanging
from the hotel balcony, protesting
as his fingers one by one are hammered,
stepped on, finally cut off with a knife.

*

"Suffering is my teacher now,"
she would say,
with a noble expression on her face,

one of the last garments in her formerly
vast Wardrobe of Affectation—

"Suffering is my teacher now" she would say—
with a noble expression on her face,
—but she kept forgetting the lesson.

      *

If the body was a traitor, yes—
it deserved to be punished,
but how could you hurt it enough, give it really
the terrible treatment required
to gratify your sense of justice?

      *

Sometimes, stationed by her bed, late at night
as she slumbered under some tonnage
of drugs and fatigue

I would feel that I was sitting in a glade
far back in the woods, a secret, verdant place
beside a hillside spring.

I could feel the pain flowing softly up
out of the bottomless dark,
seeking and finding
the aperture of her,

entering and filling it,
making its entrance
again and again

glittering and fresh
pain,
singing its song

into the light of the world.

Tony Hoagland

SUMMER NIGHT

That one night in the middle of the summer
when people move their TV sets outside
and watch them on the porch—
so the neighborhood is full of murmuring blue lights.

Earlier, the evening sky looked like a pale blue shirt
through which a stain the shade of watermelon juice
was delicately spreading.

All day I kept offering my wife
opportunities to fight,
and she kept stepping over them
like cracks in a sidewalk she was used to walking on.

Sometimes when she cries I think how
cigarettes and ice cream are part
of the chemical composition of her tears,

sometimes I think about her mom and dad,
her catastrophic history with men—
And I can feel the roots of my heart

convulse, yanking themselves up, wanting to
walk over there and hold her.

We sit in our wooden chairs,
convinced that we have ruined everything

while through the open window
comes the smell of flowers.

Christina K. Hutchins

BETWEEN HERE AND THERE

Berkeley California, for S. in Poulsbo, Washington

Does every afternoon ripen
so irrevocably?   A peach that cannot
contain its juice,
a sun that no shade tree
can tame but that bursts and bursts its skin
until millions of miles of space
cannot stop the rushing.

There was a wind off the bay
that would not be kept still
but lifted everything it could:
undulated old news along the street,
a girl's skyblue skirt,   and every hair
along my bare arm rose
until I thought we were all nearly free.

Walking home I missed you,
that quick ache
white glint of the sidewalk
    buff of wind,
and suddenly   there were a woman's desperate hands
opening against thick glass.
She was shut up

in the backseat of a police car.
    Cops standing around
trying not to see her
I wanted to stop   say to them
"Release her! Release her now!"
Wanted to go to the rolled up window

in the way the breeze
cannot hold itself

still, but empties,
empties, snapping and seeking skin,   wanted to
match my hands to hers
on the other side of the glass,

tell her, *It's all right. The air*
will move again.   Whatever
craziness is in you   on you
in from of this damn culture
you are all right.
But I couldn't, didn't do that,
don't know.

I wanted you
like June air,   the way
sunlight surges between
Mayten leaves and presses
clear through. Skin ache of my bones.
That visceral.   *This has been*
enough time between

enough of 900 miles thick
enough away from the between of your
hands. Now is time for arms
around. For us in the afternoon.   For
your fingers in mine. For skipping
weeping   juice of the day seeping relentless warm
toward dusk.

In the way the air
crowds and claims and bursts open,
the way it cannot hold
itself,   I want

you: the way
nothing is free
enough or
close enough,

in the way the woman's desperate
eyes sought me and found me,
a stranger through thick glass,
walking by,   the way
her emptying hands pressed
against the glass between us
and silently clamored through.

Mark Irwin

HEART

As he opened the sternum
I saw the heart
bubbling and red
in its cage
the working lips
of paradise
hidden in
that dark stadium
where the lion the bull
the sheep of our
desires our fears
wait over and over
it beat
like something both
epic and tired a
superman's shrunken
cape within which
another something
was wanting, waiting to
burst, spill, spell, body
over and beyond
its viscous tent.
Who now is fumbling
the reins
whipping the hide
taking me home.

Roy Jacobstein

WRITER'S BLOCK

Aground in the mire
of an evaporating waterhole
the rhino slaps the side
of his rumpled face
against the mud again
and again and again
while the little birds pick
ticks from what remains
of his good flank.

Kate Knapp Johnson

WHEELCHAIR PIROUETTE

In the best of the best
you will not find my name.
Shall I speak of disappointment?, bother

to lift one eyebrow and if so
will it be high enough?

Nor am I noted
in the least of the mediocre, stiffest
of the stiffs. No one is scouring

even a small parcel
of land looking
for me, so it will be safe, perhaps,

to take these scant
expectations, each bullet
from both temples

and place them in this plastic bowl,
carry it deep into the woods. Leaving
no crumbs. Her name

is hope. Surely
she can find her own way home.

Kate Knapp Johnson

EVERYTHING ALIVE

Even the lilacs are difficult this morning, tossing
their blues and greens so carelessly
I can hardly bear to look
at those pure shades and panicles, their tiered gowns
lifted in the moment's wind. I wanted it to be simple
to love them, but it's not. Everything alive
carries a small crucifixion inside; still,
the desire remains
to hold what's tender
impossibly close... (Oh God,

if only we had not been born
so hungry, had we not needed
the grown-ups for our very survival.... As it was,
the sheer longing of life for life
overtook us; that ardent rooting, vast
plea for relation was too much
for the world; it had to be
put away, buried within. But what hides
knows, and seeks to unveil itself
in others: what I see
is the dying face
of the lilacs, tall spears
shedding sparks of blue,
pale, unflinching blue.)

Perhaps only God can explain the reason
we tend towards that hidden, restive life, like a breeze-flown
petal, a child who wants and wants
nothing can stop the fall—into
what, who
will be there, waiting? Are we created

through our surrender
to lose ourselves in the same act? Only look
at the lilacs, parading their moony heads, unyieldingly
beautiful in the rising gusts and fog-drenched light.
I want—I will miss them
in my arms so much!

Karen Kevorkian

HUNGER

She was prepared for some things
to change once she lived by herself

for instance

no more sleeping naked.
                             Over a black slip
she wears a blue kimono
                                 its floating pink peonies
thatched in black lines like September's dry grass
along California's coast
                        where
under cattleguards
lie the crisp and negligently twisted
peeled off like a glove
or silk sweater
the woman writhes out of
skins of rattlers.

And in hills between Kowloon and China
where small houses are empty
                        everyone
moved to cities, all that's left

a garden of greens with broad leaves now forever
gone to seed
and the snake

that rears with hood flaring
whose hiss she mistakes for a cat.

The woman has favored a silver snake bangle
                               though lately
its tiny head catches sweaters.
                         Terror
is transparence
the silver snake
no armor.

What she sees from her window
a white frame building
its sides snarled with black wire
and more wire

cutting sky.

A week of hard rain
on a wall a sign appearing
                             next to
a jar of leggy carnations
                     whose petals bunched
like used Kleenex. *Goodbye Barbara*
it said

We will miss you.

The woman has on her wall
a print of a painting in Florence from the
Chiesa San Marco
a pale angel
kneeling before Mary

who inclines her head as if anxious
to catch every whisper
the paint in her lap
so faded you see the bench where she sits
though at this moment

she has not entirely
                    vanished.
Not like Barbara

who lived in the streets
of whom people remember
her bow
        palms pressed together
for the quarter dropped into her cup.

The woman passes her palm
over her black slip's silk
her belly that no longer
bears children
though it is still taut
with questions
            that Mary
at this point in the painting
not yet pregnant

or ravenous

fails to ask.

Susan Kolodny

PSYCHIATRY'S WIFE

At night the sorrows
    sift, diagnoses rearrange
themselves
      green ascends, black
        fine-powders everything
you hear yesterday's speech
    like gears, a distant
  braying. Who goes into the kitchen
  and bakes bread at 3 A.M.?
    whose yesterday skinned its knees?
I am sick to death of voices—
    mine, yours, his.
      Incessant. Plaintive.
    Begging to come in. Alms
    for the poor.
  You cannot help. When I went
    to Paris. When I go
    to Paris. When we made
      Play Doh in winter, the light
was so thin that it seemed
    sickly. The voices
    everywhere apparent, heir
      apparent. Listen!
I am sick of having
      to listen. Gregorian chants, yes.
The 3 perfect notes, a chord,
    that trembled in the air that afternoon
    in the Baptistry at Pisa.
Ringed all around by marble—
    who is the dead bride
      memorialized in stone?—
we shivered at the platinum purity

>   of the sound. The human
>   voice made flute, purified
>   of report, retort, complaint.
> I am tired now
>   of listening, more, tell me
>   more. Prey, tell.
> Comfort me, oh comfort me.
>   Listen. He told me stories
>   once, Uncle Wiggley; he was 9,
>   I was 6 or 7.
> The voice disappeared into an alleyway,
>   a narrow door, begged me to follow.

Richard Kostelanetz

RECIRCUITS

Игра суффиксами издавна ведома поэзии, но лишь в новой поэзии, в частности у Хлебникова, становится осознанным, узаконенным приемом.

Poetry has from the earliest times engaged in play with suffixes; but only in modern times, and particularly in Xlebnikov has this device become conscious and, as it were, legitimate.

—Roman Jakobson, "The Newest Russian Poetry: Velimir Xlebnikov" (1922)

ARM FARM
ROW GROW
NAP NAPE
RUN RUNE
NOD NODE
MAT MATE
LUNG SLUNG
RUDE CRUDE
LOCK BLOCK
GO GOT GOAT
LAW CLAW
RIP RIPE
EEL HEEL
LONG ALONG
RAFT CRAFT
TOKE TOKEN
LOVE GLOVE
IN KIN KIND
CENT SCENT ASCENT
AS GAS
ION ZION
RAW DRAW
NOR NORM
PAIN PAINT
LUSH FLUSH
RABBI RABBIT
RIP TRIP TRIPE
US USE FUSE

Peter Levitt

ESSAY: EVERYTHING IS PERMITTED IN THE IMAGINATION

*Often I am permitted to return to a meadow
as if it were a scene made-up by the mind,
that is not mine, but is a made place*

that is mine, it is so near to the heart
—Robert Duncan

In the meadow outside the room in which I write to you the tulips of this extraordinary spring are large enough to hold full portions of wine in their blazing red and yellow bowls. And the daffodils, with their delicate petals of pale white and gold, speak to me of the fragility all life proposes. They seem brave, somehow, determined to live to the fullest each moment they are given to live. I don't know who originally planted the bulbs that give rise to these flowers year after year but it feels as if they were geniuses of the hidden ground of my own heart and imagination, the beautiful product of their effort so speaks to me.

Imagine, for a moment, that these flowers lived in a world where permission was required for them to express through their color and form the deepest meaning of their lives. Just imagining such a world hurts the spirit all life expresses, does it not? But even in a world of such constraint permission would be granted from within each of these flowers simply by the fact that, where they are and *as they are*, there is no separation whatsoever between their existence and the means by which their lives are expressed. Red grants permission for red to exist. Yellow does the same. And it is no different for us.

Every image, dream, fantasy, thought, and all the multiple forms or ways of expressing these that come to mind in the imagination come as naturally to us as the red or golden color that comes to these flowers and therefore, like these beauties of the meadow, possess an inherent permission to exist. We cannot really take credit for the spontaneous nature of our thoughts, feelings or imaginings. They just come to us, they rise in a seeming instant from the ground of our being and often take us by surprise. They shock or delight us. They are like gifts from a friend who is either terribly loving or terribly weird, but one who seems, in the end, to know us well. So we cannot credit ourselves with these offerings, and, likewise, we cannot really accept blame for them either. They just are. If you like, consider one thought red. One image yellow. One dream may be green. Another is blue. We don't know why and so, really, as it says in the Chinese *Book of Changes*, the *I Ching*, "No praise. No blame." (One could, I think rightly, say that actions we take based on products of the imagination are of a different order and that one's personal morality might even in some way be defined by what actions we do take based on what occurs within this otherwise invisible part of our selves.) So we think what we think and dream what we dream. The unconscious mind, wherein the imagination resides, is a realm free from the usual constraints, and for reasons of its own gives us what it wants us to have at any given moment. This is the source of its permission.

It is precisely because artists have always worked hard to cultivate their ability to access and express this realm of human freedom that they have often been viewed as potentially dangerous to "the state" because "the state" prefers a particular order those in power have a stake in perpetuating. For our purposes we might consider the habits and comfort of our own ego structure as "the state." Let's call it "the state of things as they are." (Who among us has not felt a certain tremor when this state felt shaken in even the slightest degree?) As writers we do not have a stake in perpetuating even this "state." Our way is to be free from all *a priori* constraints that may have been imposed upon us by others or ourselves and to dive skyward, with a mind clear like space itself, into the fertile, open field of our own possibilities and imaginings. The greater our ability to embrace such freedom the greater our ability to know what we know, and have always known, though we may have had difficulty at times dodging the "thought patrol" in our attempt to access this knowledge through the heavy veils of constraint.

Everything is permitted
Everything is permitted
Everything is permitted in the imagination

Dear Friend, I say it again and again and again.

2.

There is a story about the T'ang Dynasty Chinese poet, Wang Wei, I dearly love. Wang had a collection of poems called *Hiding the Universe* and the question was asked, Where do you hide the universe? It's a pretty provocative question, I think, and before reading on you might offer a few answers. Where would you hide it? The answer given is one that has always delighted me with its simple clarity: You hide the universe in the universe because that's the only place big enough for it to fit. Isn't that wonderful? And the truth is that your imagination is not only vast, as vast as this universe that can only fit within itself, but it is inherently generous in all normally functioning psyches and gives you exactly what you need. Of course sometimes what your imagination thinks you need may appear, at first glance, rather extreme. It has its own way of catching our attention and some of its methods can be quite provocative. Just think about your most recent frightening or sexy dream and the confusion of feelings it called forth. But these are just some of the ways the imagination has of reeling us in so we will come closer to ourselves and eventually discover the true meaning it wants us to have, which we often only realize through the act of writing. As poet William Carlos Williams said, The poet thinks with the poem, and that in itself is the profundity.

What the imagination really wants for us only requires that we receive its gifts openly, without judgment, accepting the permission inherent in the fact of the gift itself. When we demonstrate this to our imagination through an open disposition of heart and mind, (think of receiving with an open hand as opposed to a hand closed into a fist) we cultivate the relationship we have with this part of ourselves and encourage it to continue to bring us the very treasures we truly want and need. And it will, because it knows we are really listening.

This listening is so important I can hardly write about it. When we listen deeply, giving no concern to previous notions of good and bad, right and wrong, desirable and not, we open a pathway that can take us through the unmapped territory of our own psyche, heart and spirit, and all the possible expressions these may find. This pathway is actually a lifeline or, if you will, an umbilicus to the Creative Source that is our birthright and which exists within each one of us. Once access to this connection is firmly established, and we accept the imagination's gifts *as given* and begin to find ways to express them in our writing, we are stretched, expanded by the imagination's Way to become larger than we have been. Our imagination wants us to become the true size we already are but have not yet discovered. It wants us to discover the universe of ourselves right there in the universe we already are. It is just like when Buddhists say that we are all Buddha, but still we must practice so we can truly *realize* (make real) the Buddha we are. What does it promote, *who does it serve*, when we block entry, deny permission, and turn our back on this precious gift?

One inclination I have at this moment is to ask such a simple thing of you. Why not write a sign in letters big enough for you to comfortably see, or letters whose size seems just right for now, and on this sign write only two words:

PERMISSION GRANTED

As you write these words allow everything I have written in this letter to crystallize into these two words. Let them signify your commitment to thinking and feeling with a freedom granted to you by your imagination. Let them remind you of your absolute right to free exploration and expression in your writing and in your life. Perhaps you might put this sign up beside the place where you write. Or you might make a card and carry it around and look at it when the presence of the "thought patrol" feels near. You might even let it become your mantra and chant it from time to time, but please do not forget it. Permission is granted because everything is *always* permitted in the imagination. Then, with Robert Duncan, we might conclude his poem, which comes from his book, *The Opening of the Field*:

> *Often I am permitted to return to a meadow*
> *as if it were a given property of the mind*
> *that certain bounds hold against chaos,*
>
> *that is a place of first permission,*
> *everlasting omen of what is.*

Gary Lilley

PRAYER TO SAINT JAMES BYRD
OF JASPER, TEXAS

Sometimes a sufferer wails them church blues.
She's gonna smell gin on my breath, the street
in my clothes. Her good book off the dresser
with the word stronger than the oak, stronger
than the dogwood of the cross. I have worn
misdemeanor green and cleaned right-of-ways
for the state, for a buck-fifty a day.
Where is God? I've walked boots into the ground.
Saint James, you kissed your sister at the door
and hit the road. I'm on my hands and knees
in the dry heave dawn wishing one clear eye
to see the way. Saint James take us late night
husbands, brothers, and lost sons safely home.
Lord, rebuke the rollers on their long ride.

Gerald Locklin

WILLIAM KLEIN: *CONTACT*, *NEW YORKER* PHOTO

a man with his arm around
his wife's sashed waist
disappears into the blur of
the low-ceilinged ballroom.

only his hand,
the color of her back,
remains,
and we infer his sleeve,
the color of her bodice.

optics can create such vanishings,
as can marriage.

Gerald Locklin

YOUNG CHET

for father's day my son picked up for me
this compilation from recording sessions in l.a.
in 1954 and '56,
with photos by william claxton.
was anyone ever as young as young chet?
was any white kid ever more at one
with an instrument,
with a singing voice that was not a singer's?
he didn't read music,
but i don't think dimaggio, musial,
mantle, mays, ted williams read a book
to find out what a bat was for.
swinging for them, as for chet,
the california surfer,
was as natural as easy livin'
in the good, old summertime.

and my son zach is the embodiment
of youth as well:
just finished his first year of college,
met a girl he talks to every evening,
has his first car,
first real job,
loves to see his friends but,
when they're not around,
like today, the fourth of july,
he hangs around the house with me,
both of us reading, writing,
pampering the cats,
he listening to music in his room,
and i in mine,
and sometimes to each other's.

out to lunch together.
later he'll drive over to the mall
to spend an hour joking with a friend
who has a summer job at barnes and noble.
when he gets back we walk to the market
to restore my stock of diet pepsi,
bring home a turkey sandwich for him,
stop for a video of *fight game*.
he's seen it seven times,
but this time i will watch it with him,
filling up on raisins, peanuts, cereal,
an aging father's fibered snacks.

channel surfing during breaks
we catch a *carousel* medley,
audra mc donald, from the capitol.
he's never seen it;
I insist he'll have to.
click and we're watching *yankee doodle dandy,*
another i insist he'll have to see.
(there aren't too many films
he hasn't seen, but still . . .)

my wife, his mother, has taken
the dog to the mountains to
escape the fireworks.
we'll call her in the morning.
they love each other a lot.

i'm glad he loves his father too.
i'm glad he likes me,
laughs at my jokes,
likes a number of the things i do,
is good at the few things i am good at,
and at many that i'm not.

god spare him my weaknesses, anxieties,
my limitations, awkwardness, neuroses. . .
but of course god and heredity and life
won't spare him all of them,
will maybe temper them a bit though.

may god grant him the strength to be strong
without giving hurt,
to weather the assaults of time,
of the envious,
of the damaged,
will teach him to un-knot with patience
the maddening human complications.

he is young, in love, is loved,
is bursting with love for those whose
love for him he so appreciates,
reciprocates with dividends.

he will not be young forever,
but he will always have
his having once been.

Jeffrey McDaniel

THE MIRROR IN WHICH I WILL BE JUDGED

Watching my brother get married in Golden
Gate Park, I wonder how the question got popped.

Was it like a bottle of expensive champagne,
or a big, ugly zit that wouldn't go away?

Asking a woman to marry you is like chewing
a mixture of gum and crazy glue, then blowing

a bubble. If she accepts, you stick it on the mantle.
If she declines, the bubble explodes in your face,

so you stay home for months to avoid the *hey,
what's that pink junk in your eyebrows* question?

Marriage frightens me. Not like it jumps out
from the dark and yells *boom box!* But I know

it's out there, lurking in the hills, ready to stomp
into my life in high heels, like an anti-Viking,

slamming the refrigerator door on my bad habits
and pillaging. I mean, look at my parents sit there

five apart. Staring at their fingertips, I see sparks.
Those palms made me, like a sandcastle

that didn't wash away. They fought so much
that as a child I thought my father must have

asked for her fist in matrimony by mistake.
Some small part of me wants to see *them* kiss,

or at least *how are you*? But that's not in the cards.
Heck, it's not even in the casino. The year

they quit speaking. My blood followed suit,
stopped talking as well. My Polish blood refused

to flow above my abdomen. The Irish stuff
pooled up in my chest. No, I can't ask for

a woman's whole hand in marriage. It's too much.
What would I do with such a thing—carry it

in my back pocket, like a piece of flank steak?
No, no, no. I'll downsize my request

to merely a finger. But I'll be good to that finger—
polish the knuckle each morning, draw a giant

replica of the print on my ceiling, scrub the nail
till it sparkles, the mirror in which I'll be judged,

for I know it's so much easier to be charming
to a busboy, than kind to the person you love.

Fred Moramarco

SPOTS OF TIME

How unplanned they are, arriving like wheat
in a field, dipping and swaying in the wind.
What leisure protects us from the elements?
Only terrible notes of pressure, distance, even music.
Consider April, each year another one,
slipping onto the world's stage, strutting early blooms,
making ordinary magic seem like something we can count on.
Look, there isn't any wind that comes from nowhere.
The suburban breezes are different than the howls
heard by climbers of Everest with their Sherpa guides.
My father's picture oddly gives me comfort
though he's long gone, and even the memories are fading.
Shall we say plainly what we want and simply take it?
Who is there that can soften seasons, save summer days?

Christopher Moylan

THE HILL

Outside, the cool air still
holds you, tense and sinewy,
in the laughter of blue jays.
Inside, no one sleeps anymore,
the house is unbearably clean.
In the open field, just below
the hill that blocks your view
of the city, light out of season,
air out of breath play off
the bristle of seed pods, and milk-
weed sacks, the waist-high scratch
and itch of uncut wheat waving
without sound in the shadow of
a passing jet. Most rooms
stand empty most of the time,
most rooms stand clean and white,
bleached by the stillness of
the light, the after-brightness
of a flash that will not fade
when the picture fades, vanishes.
Press your hand to the belly
of a rock, trace your fingers
on hemlock and morning-glory
climbing the quartz veins reflecting
the sunlight back to the empty
mirror above your head. The moon
swells and drops a dozen bitter
pears from a tilting tree, the sun
falls and falls like a fist on
the tallest oak, light and memory
hammered in the bark, and
the shade pools in your hand

while the sun falls. That's it,
you say, a whole day . . .
walking up the long meadow,
hand in the tall grass—traffic
whispering outside the gate
of days and days and days—
trailing your fingers
on filaments of insect wings.

Elisabeth Murawski

GLASS

Escape wraps her like a symphony half to come.
She can only imagine the smell of April.
Here are yellow bricks left over
from a war that ended too soon. And fresh
green grass too far away to tell.

To reassure she speaks her name aloud.
Petals and stems drop their rainbows
on the floor, walk her body into daylight,
into the terrors of her skin blossoming.
She moves through doors where babies are safe

and priests reveal murders of the soul
to protect the innocent. There are no exits
for desire. The blue heron folds its legs
and flies over. The gaunt freedom
in its wings' slow dance affirms

like a chill. No deliverance in sight.
She investigates the chapel
for a hint of an explanation. The sun
blazing through an art deco window
colors the host lifted up a Chinese red.

Muriel Nelson

GARGOYLE'S ANKYLOGLOSSIA

Caught
open-mouthed between fearful and fierce,

a stone,
outcast, lives

like a cat who's finished screaming
and stiffens, electrified.

One move,
just a twitch, might rub up the charge.

A whole gesture toward
you now could go wrong.

Curses, prayers and exhaust rise outdoors
like steam. Who can distinguish them,
jumbled in traffic where lights are long?

What if
from the ugliest mouth on the corner, love stuck
out its bent lightning tongue?

D. Nurkse

DRIVING WEST WITH RAGNAR NURKSE

Between Clovis and Abo
we came upon a small lake
with a fisherman in a white dinghy.
I asked the name and my father said
it's a mirage... it's always here...

Between Abo and Mesita
the identical lake,
same fisherman plying a rod
bent like a question mark,
but this time the road swerved.
Signs flashed and receded:
Thirst No More... Last Oasis...

Then the desert sealed itself
like a letter behind us
and we raced against dust.

How gorgeous his body smelled
looming beside mine:
bearing oil, lees of wine,
sweat, age, Porter's Cologne.

He had a month to live,
many minutes, infinite moments.

Often he glanced at his watch
and calculated: *Anaconda by midnight*,
and sure enough the sky opened
like a box with a secret compartment
and we entered the constellations

driving West along imaginary lines
between wavering lights,
into Spica, Deneb,
the nest of the missing sun.

D. Nurkse

THE FORMAL GARDENS AT XAIA

Loneliness had made us so crazy
we thought we were lovers,
strolling in the shadow of the fountain.

Night was falling and we might get married.
Great lamps would shine, and the flies
inch sideways into darkness.

Schoolchildren ran home laughing,
each with one life and one balloon.
A clear bell rang: the echo waited.

Delight had made us so lonely
we thought we'd leave each other,
one for the desert, one for the ocean.

The fountain was full of gum wrappers
and pennies travelers had tossed,
perhaps believing they might return

by the power of countless tiny losses
to these topiary hemlocks, this clearing,
this statue of lovers who can't turn back.

D. Nurkse

A SONG OF PACIFICATION

We bombed that parched desert
and wherever our fire fell
villages sprang up:
date palms, goat-pens, deep wells.

We mined the inner harbor
and now in dawn twilight
lovers turn back to each other,
lazy, sticky from the ocean.

How the crickets in the meadow
miss our planes
when they recede
at the speed of light
—or a shade faster—
into the white of the eye.

Louis Phillips

JOHNNY INKSLINGER JOURNEYS OUT TO THE BRONX ON THE IRT WITH JOHN DEWEY

"The local is the only universal upon which all art builds,"
John Dewey sd. as fire engines
Red-willowed thru the Bronx streets.
A tenement was on fire, children in disarray,
Women in bathrobes & curlers, black men in undershirts.
Upstairs someone was wailing "I Gotta Right to Sing the Blues."
The Local and the Express pulled into the station at the same time.
I argued for the Express; we took the local.
Arrived too late to save anybody's life.

James Reiss

MOOSEHEAD LAKE

When Brockie & I gunned
                    all ten horse
        & full-speeded
                    over a mirror
    of cloud banks
                the slap-happy
        wind
            beating time
                        on our cheeks
foreshadowed sunshine
                    & fair weather.
I could go on like this
                    rev my outboard
        & say a squall
                    blew up
    like bad news
                forcing us
        ashore
                on an island
                        where we
crouched by a beach
                under pine boughs.
I could say how it cleared
                        how Brockie
            built a campfire
                        for dried
        rice & beans
                I steamed in lake
            water
                how Spam
                        crackled
in our flame-blackened

                    Eagle Scout pan.
But if Brockie were here
                    he'd say
           none of this
                    happened
           how I cooked
                    up this whole
              mess
                    kit
                         of impressions
in my lake-haunted
                    moose-obsessed head.

Lee Rossi

DUST

The wall next door keeps rising
until finally it is all I can see.

From time to time I hear workmen
tapping the blocks
and singing beautifully in Spanish.

I step outside and there they are
six of them astride a scaffold slapping mud on top
or scraping excess from the sheer drop.
I admire their precision, pushing back space
with powerful rough hands.

And yet, rising even higher
surrounding this whole city
I see another wall.
Like insects through a hedge
we pass through it daily
finally without noticing its glittering green face.
Even as we sleep, it grows.

We are already destroyed
blonde bodies bundled in rolls
big as houses.

I cannot say who builds it.
I live as if the wall builds itself
its own father and mother.
It anchors heaven
lest God and Devil disappear.

I pray that it not fall.
I am not ready to leave this body
of theorem. I could not survive
in the black air of stars
nor enter the language of moss.

I am not ready to leave this body.
It is what I love:
this raised hand, this scream
rising to a song.

Amanda Schaffer

INEBRIOLOGY

The face grows wild with irregular
                bones and bonds, electric

like a handful of sublimated
                sea monkeys tossed in a bowl of sea:

yellow sand, yellow yolk.
                Glass is liquid, I am always

on my fifth. Do you like snow?
                It is almost Chinese New Year,

the release of the luna moth.
                Will you fall in love

with yourself all over again?
                I keep losing the left

half of every word on the tongue,
                the tang and ring. I do and don't

get cold, like snow. Most days,
                aluminum will burn and iron won't,

the bus is painted red for relevant
                and there are fencers who build

actual fences, mind-readers
                who try on mangled hairdryers

large enough for a desiccated watermelon.

Barry Silesky

MEDICINE

How much I've wanted to be brilliant, that old stupidity rising from what? Ambition, traffic, slate skies over all the beautiful women? So I'm calling her again as the walls close, and I fold into the chair, hardly breathing. But such melodrama's only another piece of the boredom, which is another word for terror. The flesh is crazy to be noticed—frantically rubbing, and brushing, dressing itself for the affair. Then I step back to look, and see there is something more important—the tube for the medicine, the place to insert the needle, the exact details of a process I've been moving toward for a lifetime without knowing. I'm late again, but I'm coming, by train, by plane, by bicycle, and she's waiting with the prescription, smiling and deadly, surrounded by the children. It's a fate more delicious than food, than the sexual scent holding me in its oily churn. Still alive, in other words. What wonderful clothes! What sleep!

Anne Silver

GOAL

The squirrel is all verb under my neighbor's oak
barbershop stripes the tree, puffed out furry cheeks
up, down
dig dig digs
to bury winter's food.

The guy with the mismatched suit but light bouncing off his
        wingtips
runs to his hump-backed Volvo
and for five minutes each morning
serenades the block
with the struggle to combust in the key of rust.

He crossed middle over pointer fingers.
This guy is a cluster of things.
I lip-read adjectives on his tight mouth
as he kicks his vintage steering wheel with a palm.

For a month now this daily drama
occurs in front of the cottage—
an add-on room
the size of a small cell block
hammered into being.

Now you know my perch,
point of view,
my job as poet is to throw a rope
lasso the elements
call them one
under the heading of making a living
perpetual nut hoarding

pretending things can be controlled by doing
or naming
acorn
needle
tree
cheek
nail hammer
I lace it all together:
we're all just swapping oxygen for carbon
carbon for air
in a nutshell:
we want full pockets, storage cheeks and publishing rights,
at least a share.

Anne Silver

UNCLE!

My family was biased by love and lilac fumes
while I was growing up.
When my folks were not kissing each other's foreheads
they were praising my brother's coin collection
and my hula-hooping.
I never had to repeat "look at me"
which accounts for my lack of dissonance, pathology.
We all folded my anklets,
pressed dad's shirts and played dominoes
in front of the fire.
Everything was done together.
Even installing the storm windows
was accomplished as a gleeful unit.
Our house faced fortunate north.
We dined on steak and chocolate cake every night
except for lobster Fridays.
My grandparents and great granny
lined their bureau tops with photos of me
in heart shaped frames.
My only sadness was the realization
I could not marry my dad
and it doesn't weigh enough.
My happy life disqualifies
any publication in the headier journals.
When I wrote about my breast cancer
I got published eight times a month.
News from the nucleus of suffering sells,
or at least gives you two complimentary copies.
From now on I lie:
I shivered under my bed
while dad ducked from flung skillets.

My brother molested my hand-me-down cat,
gunned down my mute Chatty Kathy.
I puked in the corner where granny
bled out having been poked by a burglar
with her own size 8 knitting needles.
On my way to school one day
a nun slapped me.
I wasn't Catholic.
I was a spit-wad plastered on the blackboard of life.
Now I'm better, I mean worse
and enclose an SASE,
offer first publishing rights.

Rick Smith

[ATTACH CABLE. . .]

[attach cable to the nerves. hands
and arms wet with machine oil.
goggles must be tight. leave all
writing to the machine. words stagger
out. old women from burning buildings]

Rick Smith

PEBBLE GAME

(after Cendrars and The Parker Brothers)

the child's sucker
is a moon on a stick

a broken globe
flung into a southerly
orbit

a pretense of rain
the dice tumbling
across the board
in their time

a silver gun ship
that won't float

a silver dog
the bark in progress

a top hat
a boot a
steam iron
you know the rest

the thimble protects
a girl's finger tip from
any careless prick

we have a red hotel
hollow, expensive
shoes in the hall

an unfolding white square
the children crowding in
blowing their gold

a rosy fist perforates the magnetic dawn.
it streaks across yellow sky, rolls through
pockets of radio signals in an ancient arc
to destroy a toy gone awry.

after blowing down The Arc De Triomphe
the children toss off a laugh
that shatters windows in Berlin.
we are snacks for their crazy teeth

we are underground now a
good eye is glued
to what is said to be
a star
a rock painted
on a rock

everybody says it's been raining
steadily
listen
bored little fingers
trot the boardwalk

I am a blurry
horse on fire
in the hills it
hasn't rained for months.

They are approaching The Bench tossing sacred robes and documents into space like words of praise. A guard picks up a stool. The brittle eyes of Mother Justice spill out of her stone head and roll down the marble steps like lonely planets. One bounces off an empty dog. We crouch at the mouth of July and listen for the sound. We are victims of rolling blackouts and strange ricochets.

Adrienne Su

EARLY WORK

Sometimes I think it is overly accessible.
Other times, even I have no access to it at all.

It recedes like the glove I lost on the beach, in rain
and cold, and didn't miss until the tide had come in.

At times I can push myself back into the music,
but there are too many reasons not to go back.

That night, the dog and I returned to the beach to look.
The tide, nearing the houses, left little room to walk.

Elemental melodies came in with the water,
which had its own purpose and its own meter.

The dog's damp nose twitched at everything
as she traveled not in search of anything.

Only one of us was fool enough
to hum and hunt the beach for a glove

as if the ocean could pick and choose
or be moved to mercy by a tune.

The dog made exuberant loops in the sand.
In the pocket of my coat, my cold left hand

tried to remember what it was to be warm
until we followed our fresh tracks home.

Adrienne Su

MODERNIZATION

The authorities over-organized
until everyone was a spy,

handing each other in for rewards.
No one had stockpiled VCRs

sufficiently to recognize
the lack of decent movies,

so the temple filled.
Followers were urged to build

underground pipelines
to channel their fortunes.

Soon the earth was a honeycomb
of iron, and nothing would grow.

When the tremors struck,
only money flew up.

Those who religiously followed
the bills were turned into crows,

claiming without language
their shares in the wreckage.

Virgil Suárez

TRACKS

We didn't know when
the train passed
and left the sack.

Our parents never spoke
of those gone, taken
by the police at night.

We thought of chicken
claws from roosters
our fathers brought
home from cockfights,
our mother's plucked
to make soup, talons
curved into half S's.

We thought of torture,
after all we lived in Cuba,
and people went missing.

In an attempt to find
answers, we untied
the sack from the spike,
a burlap bag, torn
in places, inside it
fingers peeked
through like tubers,
coiled in rictus,
blood-darkened,
like Fidel's teeth.

Flies buzzed there,
cicadas hissed from tall
grass and shrubs,
heat swarmed about
our legs, rose up
from the gravel, oil
stains on the rope used
to tie its mouth shut.

We opened it slowly,
thinking of worse scenarios,
a head, chopped limbs,
but no, it was simply
a bag full of fingers,
some missing nails,
clipped, sheered, jagged,
bits of flesh, gnarled
bone. Whose fingers?

We balanced ourselves
on the rails, played
at tossing rotten fingers
at each other, sang songs
on our way home.

That night we slept
with our fists clenched,
buried in our armpits.

By morning we checked
to make sure our parents
still had theirs, we ours.
We watched for signs
in people who waved
goodbye with both hands.

Elaine Terranova

DAY AND NIGHT

The rain would stop, then begin again.
In this the day was adamant.
And in between, fog,
where so much dropped out, unnecessary.

She lowered the volume
so that the radio sounded
like a little toy radio

and thought of the break
of waves, the break in a bone,
simple or compound,
like a reckless sentence.

Thought, this is how the world
is presented, swiftly, an if
from a train. At night, had almost
replaced sleep with reading,

wondering why the body means
so much, what it marks. So they

would separate, like dice cast,
not to be toted up together,
to be left anywhere they settled.

The letter, deep in his desk
or the pocket of a jacket.
He hadn't the wish or the foresight
to wad it up, milling it

between fingertips to the girth
of a split pea, and even so,
she'd have felt it
under the mattress where they lay.

Elaine Terranova

THE FIRST TIME

Last night for the first time
I dreamed I died.
But I went on living after
so I could see what this meant to the world.

For a while the shade
did not advance,
the sun didn't retreat.
It was permanent afternoon.

A train arrived at a station
and all the beautiful scenery fled
that the whole way
had been rubbing up against it.

Somewhere a man laid out
a game of solitaire
on a wrought-iron table.
Just his hands, what I saw,
and the cards.

And everywhere people stood or walked,
separate, upended, carrying
as they do
that cross in the shape
of their bodies.

There was a brittleness in the leaves,
the summer stiffening.
My eyes closed
in my dream, and an hour passed

very fast in sleep. I woke
at the slap of pigeon wings
against the red-tiled roofs.
The shade came then, and it gave

a shape to everything.
I could see I wasn't alone. Other spirits
crouched in the mountains.

Soon the same stars I remembered
would burn, they'd be
as persistent. And that was that,
night overtaking day, autumn, summer,
shadow falling over
the face of the apple.

David Trinidad

CODA TO THE "STUCK IN THE CAR" SCENE

[From "Phoebe 2002: An Essay," a continuing collaboration with Jeffery Conway and Lynn Crosbie. "Phoebe 2002" is a mock-epic based on the 1950 movie *All About Eve,* starring Bette Davis as Broadway star Margo Channing. In order to teach Margo a lesson in humility, her best friend Karen Richards (Celeste Holm) drained the gas from their car; the two sit stranded on a wintry country road. Margo will miss her evening performance, allowing her much younger understudy, Eve Harrington, to go on in her place.]

Margo need only look out the window of the car
to comprehend Williams's metaphor for "old age":

> a flight of small
> cheeping birds
> skimming
> bare trees
> above a snow glaze.

Or Plath's confrontation with "voicelessness":
"The snow has no [body with a] voice."

Compare, if you will, Williams's "Winter Trees"
with Plath's: his are "wise," "stand sleeping

in the cold"; hers "[know] neither abortions nor
bitchery," are "[t]ruer than women." And truer

friends, needless to say, than women like Karen.
The oldest tree is the oldest of all living things.

*There are trees alive today that were 3,000 years old
when Columbus first reached the shores of America.*

Yet "[e]verything dies—sooner or later." Davis
(as ancient Libby Strong in *The Whales of August,*

her first post-stroke / surgery part, as well as
her penultimate screen appearance) is there to

remind us of that; she articulates this truth as
her equally ancient co-star Lillian Gish brushes

Davis's white, Rapunzel-length hair. There are
few phenomena harder to behold than "the

harsh contortions of [B.D.'s] stroke-ravaged face."
Whales was released in 1987, two years before her

death at the age of eighty-one. James Spada
cites this frequent reaction to Davis's "withered

exterior": "Her fans . . . were shocked by her
appearance, and saddened by the knowledge

that Bette Davis was now only a weak shadow
of the energetic, no-nonsense, hell-raising Margo

Channing . . . ." Naturally Bette, no matter how
decrepit she became, never stopped swooping

about on her broomstick. A feud too geriatric
to be deemed divine developed between Davis

and Gish. Spada: "When someone commented
that Lillian looked wonderful in a close-up, Bette

snapped, 'She *ought* to know about close-ups.
Jesus, she was around when they *invented* them!'"

On another occasion, Davis proclaimed, "You try
working with a deaf mute!"—a more than unkind

jab at Gish's poor hearing. Two years prior
to filming *Whales,* the anile actresses were both

present at an awards ceremony. Gish went onstage
to deliver a "lovely but lengthy" speech about

D.W. Griffith. As she rambled on, Davis, who was
seated in the front row, began to mutter out loud,

"The silly bitch, get her off, get her off." Feeble
imbroglios aside, is it possible to view Davis's

extremely visible deterioration as a gift? Few,
if any, contemporary actresses are able to age for us

the way Davis aged—a truly generous and courageous
choice, despite her egomaniacal drive? How many

stars have "lifted" themselves beyond recognition:
Faye Dunaway, Melanie Griffith, Cher. Celebrities

are being replaced at an ever-accelerating rate;
Warhol's "fifteen minutes of fame" will be whittled

down, eventually, to a mere fifteen seconds. In
many ways, Anna Scott, the character played by

Julia Roberts in the recent film *Notting Hill,* is
today's Margo Channing. "Not long from

now," predicts the thirty-something superstar,
"my looks will go. They will discover I can't act.

And I will become some sad, middle-aged woman
who looks a bit like someone who was famous

for a while." That Scott / Roberts should have this
wistful insight at age thirty (in contrast to the crisis

Channing / Davis experiences at "four oh") indicates
an unmistakable shortening of celebrity life spans.

Stars of the future won't have to worry about aging;
they won't be in the spotlight long enough *to* age:

before the wrinkles, before "that indefinable slack-
ness in the skin" requires surgery, they will have

been supplanted by Phoebe 2000, Phoebe 2001,
Phoebe 2002. Retire young, stay pretty—as Garbo's

filmography attests (unlike the late-in-life paparazzi
shots scattered throughout the tabloids, cf. Bardot's

"spoiling fruit"). "Age settled with more grace on
ordinary people, but for celebrities—women stars

in particular-age became a hatchet that vandalized
a work of art." *Jackie Susann, she meant it that way.*

William Trowbridge

COACH SAID

no water during practice. You don't wanna end up
like the guys in those movies, lost for days
in the desert and then they find the oasis and guzzle
away with nobody there to stop em. They think
their luck's finally changed, that the world's just
turned into Momma's tit, but they get water-logged
and die. I saw a man die in the war—bang, like that—
the start of training, run over by the bus that brought us,
and I don't want to see it again, no sir. It can spoil
a good marriage, seeing that. So don't let me find
anybody sneaking water. Use the salt tablets. And no
dissipation the night before a game—"shooting your wad"
to you comedians in the back. It drains vital fluids,
same as crying. You're left with an unfocused mind
and a case of cotton mouth. Take some extra laps if
you're so hot and bothered. Jump in a cold whirlpool.
Don't expect to be some Romeo stud, who thinks
his little cheerleader won't spit on him when he's down.
I could tell you some things, but just remember this:
It ain't gonna be like last year. No goddamn water.

Lee Upton

ROMAN BATHS

Rust in the walls,
        somehow as if the walls
were a garage
        more recently than
a Roman bath.
        But here the Romans
scaled themselves,
        took their libations
in the steam of their
        complicated passions.
Fog pours in from the
        roofless stadium.
The Romans discharged
        their waters in a shunt
to the underworld,
        a crevice now in a
rainfall of sludge.
        Why, as a young woman,
didn't I linger here
        to imagine the Romans
flinching with their
        ancient errors,
even to see the Romans
        bathing in salts
from the sea and secured
        by two
at a minimum
        corners of the world?
Ignorance, it is an empire.

Amy Uyematsu

THESE UPHELD ARMS

There are days when nothing matters more than the trees I pass on my afternoon walk. An unexplained comfort in the denseness of their leaves, the formidable shadow a solitary tree can make though surrounded by taller buildings. Lately I notice the trees on my street. Sidewalks twist and split from the pressure which keeps building underneath. Many grow too rapidly, enveloping the city's fluorescent lamps and making night more dangerous.

Quietly I celebrate a tree that looms so large its branches span the entire width of the street, filling the air with cool, fragrant shade. I find myself drawn to the curve and substance of roots as they spread from the thickening trunk. How satisfying to imagine the slow, sinuous limbs and fingers, all reaching toward water and light. Then descend through the very core of the tree, follow the labyrinth of roots snaking back to the moist buried stem.

More than ever before, my aging hands resemble a tree. Sometimes my lover watches me in my sleep and later asks what I've been dreaming. No longer an occasional gesture, I awaken to find myself lying on my back, palms open, both arms raised like branches, my face to the sky. Next to me he lies on his side, legs and arms tucked in. Lately I wonder what our bodies are telling us, even as we sleep.

Amy Uyematsu

SUKOSHI / LITTLE BITES

call me
frivolous
I can look
for days
at that pale
green
cup

~~~

each rain
drop grows
louder?
no, hear
the drown of
my heart

~~~

amazed
by one more
season, mother's
string beans
so crispy
and sweet

~~~

the sound
of white moving
blue, a ripple
of one
awakened

~~~

you ask
the oak
I'll smell
the pine
our preference
becomes us

David Wagoner

ON BEING ASKED TO DISCUSS POETIC THEORY

I know for a fact snow falls in the mountains.
    I've stood there while it fell
        On me and the temporarily bare stones.
I could see it falling into the broken baffles
    Of granite, hovering on the edge
        Of thawing or staying frozen, both joining
And withholding itself from its other self
    At the confused beginning of spillways
        And misdirected channels and transparently
Aimless pools while it gathered
    And went less often in the wrong directions,
        And I've followed the water down (like it, with no need
To remember where I was or what I was)
    And stood beside its mouth on the ocean shore
        And looked back at the source,
At that stark whiteness. If it all disappears
    Behind clouds this winter, I can be certain
        That where I climbed those steeper and steeper miles
Along its path to the end of trees, to the end
    Of crouching shrubs, to the last of the tendrils
        And wild flowerheads, the same snow is falling.

David Wagoner

IN THE FOG

That evening, they walked in fog, trying to be
    Romantic about it, though not over-fond
        Of their own confusion. They could see almost
Ten yards ahead and around them
    And, overhead, the near equivalent
        Of the zero underfoot. They thought they knew
Where they were as well as they knew each other.
    They recognized that street, that concrete sidewalk,
        Even their neighbor's trees like the palms of their hands.
They could have bet their lives they were something less
    Than fifty yards from home. Their memories
        Assured them it was there, beyond that vapor
Rolling in from the sea and interfering
    With the remains of sundown. If they had kept
        Standing there, if they hadn't moved
Forward then, they'd never have known
    What they know now. They took one hesitant step
        Together and another and quickly two more
And two more and even began
    Strolling along toward the virtual semblance
        Of what they thought was theirs. They wanted to see
So they could believe again. But daylight
    Or dark, in every weather since, stark sunlight
        Or moonless midnight, that whiteness follows them.

David Wagoner

GOOD NIGHT

You can't get excited about going to sleep.
   —Roethke, *Straw for the Fire*

But you can, and if you do, expecting
         Altogether too much from one tomorrow,
                  You can wrap your head in a good old-fashioned
Nightcap and be ear-plugged and eye-shaded
         And pillowed and nest-egged over and under down,
                  Sheeted and blanketed and comforted
And made to feel as little
         As possible, so you'll hear nothing new or erroneous
                  Like your own preambles and prefaces, the squeaks
And rumbles of the overture
         To that tone poem for basso and soprano,
                  Uvula ostinato, and start flying
To the four unearthly corners of your eyes. Oh,
         Yes, you can get excited, but stark awake,
                  No one will want to be near you when you go
Or when you arrive in a heap at the other side
         Of that bad night or hear you greeting the dawn
                  With disappointment under the Xmas tree,
Tearing apart the glittering, breakable presents
         As savagely as the child you were or the bear
                  You are, spreading himself at the picnic table.

Jesse Waters

A NEW WALK

—for A.R. Ammons—

Albert Goldbarth asked me to name
a great poet on the Wednesday
before you died, and I forgot you
and said, "John Milton."

It's true, I'd loved Milton
longer than you, and given the island
and one book only, well . . .

Your death could not be simple for me
like Milton's, imagined and dry
as gold leafed pages in leather:

gone while I was watching something else:
The wild yellow daises, honeysuckle bushlimbs,
fluvio-glacial deposits, scattered cedarcone
I could only see, and not smell: Fine,
brown seedlings ground to grist: The silent offering
of your death.

But it isn't time to let things be,
to let the draft-books fall—
the song's improvident center
in me, still in you, still assures
the self that is ours, all of ours:
a new walk is a new walk.

Charles Harper Webb

PURPLE COW

—I never saw a purple cow, I never hope to see one...

Its lack was my first hint that life wasn't
endless possibility—that lima beans turned
to ice cream, and Baptist choirs sang "Teddy
Bear's Picnic" only in cartoons and dreams.

As I curled in Mommie's lap, reason whirred
away, grinding my plan to find Alladin's lamp
thin as the chance that I'd replace Willie Mays,
or wed my babysitter, Bonnie Hines.

I didn't think about that, though.
I thought about cows of all colors but purple
strolling up to My-T-Fine Foods,
holding bottles of the cold milk they "gave."

I never thought that every touch
of Mommie's hand, every repetition
of her rhyme shoved me away from childhood's
surrealist play toward high school

melodrama, then the naturalism
of adult life, where a rose is a rose,
a bad job is a bad job, a resentful wife
is a resentful wife exclusively—

where no corpse is exquisite, and the pits
of neurosis and anomie yawn, vast
as the number of things I'll never do,
never in my life so much as hope to see.

Charles Harper Webb

BEING CHARLES H. WEBB, PH.D.

*Every morning upon awakening, I experience a supreme
pleasure: that of being Salvador Dali.*
—from *The Journal of a Genius*

Every morning upon awakening, I experience a supreme
ambivalence. As I pull on longjohns for a fishing trip,
or lie still, savoring the slosh of rain on a do-nothing Saturday,
I can't forget how past alarms have yanked me, fish-like,
out of sound sleep into corrosive air. Sometimes
I practically prance at my desk, sure of my worth,
not caring that the NEA hurls cash at everyone but me.
Other times I'm like a man who's spent his life writing
a novel called *Bad Brie*. When life's cold shovel smacks
my knees, groin, head, then starts to bury me, I ache to be
Dali, my every action Art. I tell myself his egotism was a pose

that felt, sometimes, like red-hot armor worn over longjohns
soaked in centaur blood. But what soothes most is to recall
that he's stopped waking, while I still climb out of bed:
a non-genius who isn't snorkeling or fly-fishing enough,
but is still able to admire a purple couch sprawled on its side
beneath dead plants that hang like Dostoyevsky beards
down my neighbor's tan retainer walls—still able to applaud
my heartbeat's rose blooming sixty times a minute,
oxidation crackling in every cell as I walk outside
to where one corner of my *Times* flickers like fire in wind—
still curious, when I heft each new morning's edition, what I'll find.

Roger Weingarten

INTO THE MOUTH OF THE RAT

—My Father's Skin

Into the hotel shower to scald
the plane ride and the terror
of seeing him and Stepmother
out of my pores, out of the years
of pretending he possessed even a penny's
worth of love for me. Into the no man's land
behind the flimsy curtain of my
resolve not to let them
get to me, I remember my uncle, once my
old man's business partner and confidante,
describing him over blintzes and stewed
prunes: Roger, your dad never
made a bad deal and never loved a soul outside
his own skin. I drive under the jackknifed
security gate, under orange trumpets
of hibiscus hedge, under sun-bleached
tile roofs and palm fronds like twirling skirts
over green coconuts that remind me of his
custom-made silver and jade cock
and ball key ring: rabbinical
seminarian, self-made
cuckold, survivor of a twelve-year
string of surgeries, proud owner of a powder
blue Rolls and a diamond pinkie, you can bet
that I'm his first born passing a convoy of golf cart
drivers and great birds corkscrewing
their necks to take a gander at this interloper
turning a rented red Mustang
into the Guest space. A chameleon
scurries over stucco. The doorman's stare

starts at my shoes and works its way like a patient
lover to my buckle embossed with the word
plumber amidst a bouquet of tools. I step out
of the mirrored world of the service
elevator snapping shut like a guillotine
turned sideways. My old man propped on pillows
stares out of his chemical tan at the miniature
Republican ex-governor on TV pretending
to be president. The nurse
shakes my hand and her head when Stepmother,
at the top of her voice, says, Mike, it's Roger.
When I lean to kiss his forehead, he uses
my cover to slide his right hand over his left
to pick at a scab over a raised dark blue vein.
I take the slender hand in both of mine,
and massaging the transparent
skin around it with my thumbs,
stare into the demilitarized
zone of his eyes and wonder—after having
his secretary fire my brother
over the phone, all to meet the requirements
of the second wife and his need to strike
back at the first—how he could live
with himself. Dad, I ask out loud, surprising
myself, do you understand? Squeezing
my finger curled under his palm, he looks—curious,
loving, who can tell— into my version
of his brown eyes. The nurse
wants to know, has he always
been this passive. Stepmother charges
the bedroom in a flurry of arms
and sobs, shrieking
my Mikey, my Mikey and pulls the black and blue,
scabbed, scarred and cratered
rag doll to her sleepless kisser,
kissing him like a wounded child,

while he struggles to purse
his lips to get a kiss in, then his eyes
close and he falls
out of the moment
into a defensive
sleep.

—Shaving My Father

The nurse wheeling him into the master bath a la mode
the hall of mirrors at Versailles, confides she can feel
her ulcer when she lifts him. Together, we prop
his upper torso on knife-thin legs she tells me
will never again support what's left
of his life, and, gripping his puppet arms,
we strip the urine-soaked diaper,
shimmy him through another door
onto a plastic potty with raised sides strapped
over the porcelain throne in his private stall,
where he relieves himself
and falls asleep. How long
can he survive like this? He'll be in a coma
in a week, so if you want to see him again,
don't leave. In slow motion, brushing
his own teeth, he spits into the brass hole
in the green marble sink, takes the razor
out of my hand just as the phone rings,
brings it to his ear, and in the torn,
paper-thin rasp I can't get used to, asks
the razor, Who's calling? I take it back,
push the button, lift the skin on his neck,
and recall my uncle, decades ago, shaving
his father, a retired carpenter, with a brush
and lather, a scene more beautiful
than any Mary washing the body of Christ.
I scrape the hidden blades across
his delicate skin.

— In Their Apartment

Stepmother easing father into the recliner
next to the easy chair, where I'm deep
into John Irving's *A Widow for One Year,* says Roger
everyone still blames you for his heart attack,
but—she bends to kiss the top
of his pale sleeping skull— we can still be pals
when this is finished. At least you'll have
half a family. Brewing my own
mixture of outrage and guilt, I blurt,
Thanks. I'm sorry if I ever
hurt either one of you, wondering
how the other half died on the battlefield
of her imagination, this aging warrior/stepmother,
her vodka-and-cake-bloated gut, breastless, flesh
of her arms dangling like melted armor, always,
even in her shark-like sleep, devising
ways to divide her enemies. I'll never
forget my ex—in bed with her semi-
secret lover—calling me after midnight
at the Midwest Writers Conference for the deaf,
dumb and blind to tell me my father,
who I hadn't spoken to for a year of blame-
filled silence, had been driven
on his back to the hospital. My last words:
Don't stuff your wife
down my throat, counterpunching
his battering ram of accusations, hanging up
on him and Stepmother breathing
through her mouth on the other phone
in their apartment.

    I can fly back at a moment's notice.
What are you talking about, she replies.

          You know what I mean—why make it hard?
You father's brother's in charge of all
arrangements.
          Are you saying my uncle, who doesn't
          even speak to his children, will decide
          whether I'm allowed to attend
          my father's funeral?
You'll have to get an even
shorter haircut, unwrinkle your clothes,
make sure your brother doesn't
show his face—and don't talk crazy
to my friends. [Which reminds me
of her monologue while driving my father,
his nurse— who told me Stepmother
didn't have a friend— and me to the promised land
of the beach.] They removed polyps
from his rectum in January, '98. . . He underwent
a quadruple bypass in the summer, followed
by a double hernia and a softball-
sized growth cut out of his abdomen
after Labor Day. This
is where I buy your father's
monogrammed hankies—where Whatshername
owns the top three floors—no one
shops here anymore— you can get
AIDS from a baked potato
in that restaurant because illegal
aliens handle them— and both his knees
replaced in winter turned
into an endless rehab—he would have died
without me—then that tumor
attacked his brain—I discovered it, telling
the doctors they were all
full of it, chemo, the first
pneumonia, electric stimulation for
his vocal chords torn by tubes

snaked down his throat so what little
food he could eat wouldn't fall
into a lung. Now that the tumor's
back in business, do you think
they should operate—it's queer to roll
your shirtsleeves more than twice, never
above the elbow. Look at you. You could
have visited once a year—no one believes
your girlfriend's Jewish—don't open
your window for charity workers
working the streets. Even if they're dressed
like Santa, they're all
drug addicts.

    I've got to leave.
But your plane's not for hours. You can't
say goodbye, he's asleep on the balcony.

I signal the nurse next to him
reading a romance novel
to give us a minute. Remembering
my stepsister explaining the first night
I arrived how my father had been
almost deaf since forever, which
is why, she said, they shout at him, I lifted
his chin up, buried in his chest, asked
in a whisper if he could hear me. He
squeezed my hand
lightly.
I put everything—fifty years of needing
this mysteriously
disappearing hero of my heart, who
put his arm around me in May of 73 and said
Everything's all right.
I put everything I've got: my only memory

of all of us around the table,
where my father kidding my brother
threatens to take off his belt
to punish him, when my mother, over a forkful
of Spanish tongue and succotash, says
Then your pants will fall down.

I put everything I've got left in me—
how he tried with a tough guy look
on his face to answer my son, who wanted
only to know why his grandfather wouldn't speak
for a lifetime to his own daughter—
everything into a last
I love you, Dad.
His lips move.
His eyelids droop.
I close the screen door behind me.
Awkwardly,
I hug Stepmother leaning
on both elbows into the kitchen
island, but she's
not having any.

I'll walk out on the balcony, she says, and watch
as you drive away.

Kathleene K. West

"END THE HEARTBREAK AND EMBARRASSMENT OF TERRIBLE COFFEE FOREVER" OR WHY MY TWIN SISTER BECAME A RADICAL FEMINIST

—from Farberware coffeemaker ad in *Seattle Times*, 11/25/73

What good is it
if you dazzle him
with your Shrimp Marengo,

strike him dumb
with your Rum Torte
and then disappoint him
with a so-so cup of coffee?

It's no good,
that's what it is.

But now there's hope. In fact
there's even more than hope.
There's the Farberware Superfast
fully automatic coffeemaker.
In addition to making coffee very fast
it makes coffee very good.
And all you have to do
to make perfect coffee
every time is to spoon
the correct measurements of coffee
into your Farberware coffeemaker.

Which we're sure you can manage
nicely, knowing as you now do
that it can turn

your only culinary failure
into yet another triumph.

Now's the time to act.

Destroy your present coffee pot.
Or give it to a close enemy.
Then go and get yourself
a Farberware automatic coffeemaker.

And get back to the business
of living happily ever after.

Eve Wood

REVIEW:
GOD by DEBORA GREGOR
Penguin, 2001. $16.00

In Debora Gregor's book *God*, the dead poet is likened to the all-knowing creator, the diviner of weeds and golf courses, only to fall into a staid and troubled consciousness, battling a private crisis of self even in the face of creation. Gregor's God tells us to "make straight a highway down the beach where Hell's Angels slouch / toward Daytona to be reborn," her heaven populated by a complicated assembly of oil barons who could be angels in crisis, beating their wings at the crossroads between heaven and self imposed greed, and the librarian who "stabs a pencil into her hair," unable to forge a human connection. God is "tired of being a God," assaulted by the obvious, strangely betrayed by His own imaginings, unable to share them with anyone or anything because the world takes His name in vain "at the sand trap of the water hazard / of the Fountain of Youth Gold Course." The world refuses complexity, grief, its own inherent beauty, all of which God has made possible, opting instead for Bingo.

The poems in this collection are like desperate shouts inside a long cave, inciting the dark to gather itself and rise up, yet drawing comfort finally in echoes, in the residue of a voice, which is God and the figure of the dead poet, and each person marked by longing, by dreams sustained in solitude, and ultimately the impulse toward beauty, toward the desire to imagine, to create. The most engaging poems in this collection explore not a literal creation, but imagination into art. In "Memoirs of A Saint (after Magritte)" Gregor implores us not to "look at that cloud—/ it has breasts!" This line is both humorous and seductively playful. Gregor tells us she "walked through the valley // of the shadow of the breast hidden / in the spelling lesson" and found she feared her own body. The poem appears satirical yet embodies a mordant personal honesty.

Gregor's God embraces loss and tries, despite Himself, to describe that loss back to us, to celebrate it, and ultimately to translate for the world what He knows of loneliness, "having never been that far east before," yet willing to travel as far and for as long as is necessary.

Gail Wronsky

DE GROTESCO

Even though I live in the woods I am not
a wolf. I know
that this portrait requires   a poetry
somewhere between the music of
Piazzola and Liszt.   A single,
            elegant pelican between
the water and your brow.

As air is absorbed by plants, as
the parody of art is   beneath
contemplating
            when we're hungry,

always I am haunted by the sad lying of
interpersonal indifference.   What if

eternity is virginal? Who would be candid
            enough to approach it?
Who would return to the palisades
of paradise   and not be
            scandalized? As with
love
    we have to give ourselves. We
have to marvel among oddities—and swoop,
        and dive, and devour.

Gail Wronsky

DE CRIMINAL

At the beginning   it was simple—
animal vulgarities. I knew better.

You knew better.   To make sense
of things   nowadays,   the

quiet, the dark, the anarchism of our
primary   relationships,

we continue. Distracted by flowers,
by tinfoil.   We say

to be happy is to be without memory.
We say   no man or woman

can be compensated for the nights they
favored a particular euphoria

beyond its means.   That is, of course,
the   interminable   orchestra

of envy   you hear,   elevating
our arcane posturings, *encore*-ing

nostalgia,   imitating our m.o.s, our
getaway icicles.

Gail Wronsky

DE MUSE

Ah, the well-known lyrical décor!
Headphones,   blindfold, and her famous
Alsacian purifications. Guilty

of love   the springtime offers
azaleas. Guilty   of beauty, the
nighttime sends its   gold-eyed owl.

Who can be blamed?   We judge her
pettily in spite of   corresponding throbbings
of the pubis.   She's

fat as a sunset, we say,   knowing
nowadays   there's nothing more unfortunate
than amplitude of hide.   She's

greasy as a melancholy   rhyme. What
self-esteems are   each day, paradoxically,
dismantled   in her beehive?

For all we know, she's fucking someone else
right now   in the privatest spaces
of our   high, sepulchral minds

and he is sobbing   like crazy, like an
exquisite fountain.   His ecstasy
what's keeping us alive.

Dean Young

REDUX TELEMACHUS

This night sky: not easily understood
by even the post-celebrities in black
silk who never come out any other time,
taking up the best table, obviating,
so miserable it seems unfair they aren't
already dead and really famous.
Most fun I've had lately's been
turning off TVs in a giant electronics shop.
Too soon the staff was on to me,
hastening my withdrawal with promises
to consider satellite. Indeed
a personal connection to a charged
object rotating in outer space gives one
a new confidence, perhaps making up
for the father never found. I feel
I can now merge and exit at will,
using my blinkers when I damn well please
but still I cannot say the name
of my favorite song. It just comes on
and just as swiftly fades, broadcasters
shouting about fetal stem cell harvest,
new embargoes to give the suicide bombers
something to write home about.
There is no one I can ask
yet the answers linger under rocks
where they always are if you can find
the right rock and not be stung.
Happened once to a cousin of mine
who didn't know wasps had an entrance there.
Who would? A simple dithyramb seemed appropriate
although prompt medical attention
would have been a plus. Next week

is Bring Your Pet to Work Week
and I realize we have just met but
would you mind if I stuck my nose
in your crotch? The hours whip
and I am sorely chased.

Dean Young

PRAYER TO A WINDOW

Of some people all that remains,
I wouldn't call it a flash,
more like a purposefully broken bottle
or saying, I pray to a window.

I was looking at a naked girl
in my shower and all I can see
is her ring that flips over, one side
a lion in lacquer, not what's on the other,
her trying to say something that's not getting past
the sizzle of my forgetting her.
We're too young.
Even a year after the accident,
I'd walk down the alley
and still get it wrong.

I remember tearing out a page
but not what I did with it.
Something I wanted for later,
some words I didn't know the meaning of
ergo musical. "Window" repeated a lot
although I remembered that about "raincoat"
in something else and was disproved.
You can't find things
and then when you do
that just accentuates losing them.
Are you with me? Forever.
It's okay if you're not.

I'm not sure what I'm doing.
Look at everything happening now.
Detailed masques of solidity,

precision of raindrops to general effect.
Whole songs. Prayer to a window—
what could that mean? Atomically

there's not a lot to stop one thing
from passing through another but not
here. I'm walking home a different way
during rush hour. Two women crouching
over a deer that's been hit. Still
breathing but you could touch its open eye.

Dean Young

EMBRYOYO

I don't ask for much: a little cleavage,
the honey of deconstruction to go along
with my cereal but something's scorched
my curtsey, one of my eyes's funny.
For the Incredible Shrinking Man,
the problem is living in your wife's
dollhouse then fighting an arachnid
with a safety pin then the really strange
problem of existence when you're smaller
than the atom which the end of the movie
makes look like new galaxies the credits
roll over. The phone rings at 4, 3, 2, 1.
The cable guy finds the body.
This is a test, only a test. The students
charge from the basements armed with pop
bottles of kerosene. Tanks were the problem
for the Incredible Colossal Man too,
and megalomania but it's not what you see
when you look into the mirror, it's what
the mirror sees looking into you. I feel
like I'm at the end of something—
my garment bag's about to burst.

Contributors

RONALD ALEXANDER's poems and stories have appeared in many journals. His novel, *The Final Audit*, was recently published by Hollyridge Press. He lives in Venice, CA.

JACK ANDERSON is the author of nine books of poetry, the most recent of which *Traffic: New and Selected Prose Poems* (New Rivers Press, 1998) won the Marie Alexander Award for Prose Poetry. He is also a dance writer and serves as one of the dance critics for the *New York Times* and the New York correspondent for *The Dancing Times* of London.

MARCIA ARRIETA is a native of Los Angeles. She has been published in numerous journals, including *Tinfish, Score, Xtant, Gestalten, Heaven Bone, So To Speak, Lost & Found Times, American Writing, Furrow, Jabberwock Review*, and *Sulphur River Literary Review*. Her chapbook, *Experimental:*, was published last year by Potes & Poets Press. She has edited and published the poetry journal *Indefinite Space* for the last ten years.

BARRY BALLARD's poetry has most recently appeared in *Quarterly West, The Chariton Review*, and *New Delta Review*. His collections include: *Green Tombs to Jupiter* (Snail's Pace Press Poetry Prize) and *Charred Fragments of Light* (Creative Ash Press Poetry Prize).

AMIRI BARAKA is a prolific writer of poetry, criticism, fiction and drama. His work includes *Wise Why's Y's: The Griot's Tale* (1995) and *Funk Lore: New Poems (1984-1995)* (1996). The illustrations that accompany his poems are his own. He lives in New Jersey.

BRUCE BEASLEY's fourth book, *Signs and Abominations*, was published last year by Wesleyan University Press. He has new work appearing in *Grand Street, Harvard Review, Kenyon Review*, and other journals. He teaches at Western Washington University.

MOLLY BENDALL's most recent book of poems is *Dark Summer* from Miami University Press, 1999. A new collection, *Ariadne's Island*, will appear in Spring 2002. She teaches at the University of Southern California.

RICK BURSKY lives in Los Angeles. His work has appeared in many journals including *Harvard Review, Epoch, Verse, Quarterly West, Poem, Shenandoah* and *Black Warrior Review*.

JUSTIN ISRAEL CAIN flirts with the Gatha of Impermanence. MFA from Vermont College. Voted most likely to.

TOM CHANDLER is the State Poet Laureate of Rhode Island, and was the 1998 Brown University Phi Beta Kappa Poet. His work has appeared in *Poetry*, *The New York Quarterly*, *The Atlanta Review* and many other journals. His third collection, *Wingbones*, was published in hardcover by Signal Books.

TRICIA CHERIN teaches English, Humanities and Interdisciplinary Studies at California State University at Dominguez Hills, where she has also served as Chair of Women's Studies and Writing Lab Director. Currently, she is Local Activity Director for the Department of Education Title V grant on her campus. Her poems have appeared in *Chiron Review*, *American Poets and Poetry*, *Cider Press Review*, *Psychopoetica*, *Old Crow Review*, *Pearl*, *Spring: The Journal of the E.E. Cummings Society*, *Home Planet News*, and *Wormwood Review* among others. She has been nominated twice for a Pushcart Prize.

NELS GOÑI CHRISTIANSON is a native of Merced, California. He is fluent in Spanish and Portuguese, and lived for two years in Brazil. He has travelled widely in South America. His poems have appeared in *WestWind*, *Verve*, *Poetry L.A.*, *Sculpture Gardens Review*, and *Valley Contemporary Poets*.

ANN COLBURN is a teacher and poet living in Los Angeles.

WANDA COLEMAN's poems recently appear in *Poetry New Zealand*, *Paterson Review* and *River Styx*. Her books include *Imagoes*, *Heavy Daughter Blues*, *African Sleeping Sickness*, *Hand Dance*, *American Sonnets* and *Bathwater Wine* for which she received the 1999 Lenore Marshall Prize presented by the Academy of American Poets, the New Hope Foundation and *The Nation* magazine. *Mercurochrome: New Poems* was published by Black Sparrow Press in 2001.

PATRICIA CORBUS' poems have appeared in numerous journals, including *Green Mountains Review*, *Folio*, *Antigonish Review*, the *Wallace Stevens Journal*, *Greensboro Review*, *South Carolina Review*, *Cream City Review*, *Paris Review*, *Antioch Review*, *Georgia Review*, *Iconoclast*, *Cincinnati Poetry Review*, and *Kestrel*.

MARY CROW has published four collections of poems, including *I Have Tasted the Apple* (BOA, 1996) two chapbooks, two full-length collections, and five works of poetry translation. Individual poems have appeared recently in

American Poetry Review, Ploughshares, Field, Alaska Quarterly Review, The Massachusetts Review and *Quarterly West*. Currently, she is Poet Laureate of Colorado and teaches in the creative writing program of Colorado State University.

DARIA DONOVAN has been published in *ONTHEBUS*. She lives in Los Angeles.

ANNIE FINCH's books of poetry include *Eve* (Story Line, 1997); *Marie Moving* (forthcoming, 2002); *Calendars* (a 2000 National Poetry Series finalist), and a translation of the complete poems of Renaissance poet Louise Labé. She has also written and edited numerous books on poetics including *The Ghost of Meter*; *A Formal Feeling Comes: Poems in Form by Contempoerary Women*, now in its sixth printing; and *An Exaltation of Forms: Contemporary Poets Celebrate the Diversity of Their Art*. Her work has been published in journals and anthologies including *Paris Review, Kenyon Review, Partisan Review, Poetry, Yale Review, Thirteenth Moon, Field,* and *(How)ever*. She is Associate Professor at Miami University of Ohio.

STEWART FLORSHEIM's poetry has been widely published in small press periodicals and anthologies. His poetry appeared in many magazines including *Double Take, Slipstream 19,* and *Rattle 14*. His work is included in the anthologies *Unsettling America: Race and Ethnicity in Contemporary American Poetry* (Viking Penguin, 1994), *And What Rough Beast* (The Ashland Poetry Press, 1999), and *Bittersweet Legacy* (University Presses of America). He is the editor of *Ghosts of the Holocaust* (Wayne State University Press, 1989), an anthology of poetry by children of Holocaust survivors. His essay, "Protecting the Angels," will appear in the anthology, *Voices from the Couch*.

CHRIS FORHAN's work has been published recently in *Poetry, Parnassus, New England Review,* and *Ploughshares*. His book *Forgive Us Our Happiness*, winner of the Bakeless Poetry Prize, was published in 1999 by University Press of New England, and a long poem, "*x*," was published last year by Floating Bridge Press.

RICHARD P. GABRIEL is a poet, essayist, and computer scientist. His most recent book is a collection of essays called *Patterns of Software: Tales from the Software Community*. *Work in Progress: Writers' Workshop and the Work of Making Things* is expected out in Fall 2001 from Addison Wesley Longman. His manuscript, *Leaf of My Puzzled Desire*, was a finalist for the National Poetry Series.

LOUIS GALLO's fiction, poetry and essays have appeared, or will appear soon, in such journals as *Glimmer Train, New Orleans Review, Mississippi Review, Missouri Review, Mangrove, Louisiana Literature, Black River Review, Italian Americana, Reversledge, Rockford Review, Habersham Review, Greensboro Review*, and others.

RICHARD GARCIA is the author of *The Flying Garcias* (University of Pittsburgh Press) and *Rancho Notorious* (BOA Editions). His poems have recently appeared in *Mid-American Review, The Colorado Review*, and the anthology *Urban Nature*, published by Milkweed Press. He is poet-in-residence at Children's Hospital in Los Angeles, assisted by a series of grants from the California Arts Council and the Johnny Mercer Foundation.

SHIRLEY GRAHAM's work has been published in various poetry magazines, including *Santa Monica Review, California Quarterly, Poet Lore*, and the *National Poetry Competition Winners*.

JULIE GRASS is a poet living in Los Angeles. Her poems have appeared in *Northwest Review, Sojourner, Hawai'I Review, PMS*, and *Eureka Literary Magazine*.

WILLIAM GREENWAY's sixth collection of poetry, *Simmer Dim*, is from the University of Akron Press Poetry Series, as is the forthcoming anthology *I Have My Own Song For It: Modern Poems of Ohio*, which he is co-editing with Elton Glaser. His publications include *Poetry, Southern Review, Poetry Northwest, American Poetry Review, Shenandoah*, and *Prairie Schooner*. He won the 2001 Ohioana Poetry Award, the 1997 Larry Levis Editors' Prize from *Missouri Review*, the 1993 Open Voice Poetry Award from The Writer's Voice, the 1993 State Street Press Chapbook Competition, and was 1994 Georgia Author of the Year. He is Professor of English at Youngstown State University.

SUSAN HAHN is the author of four books of poetry, all published by the University of Chicago Press. She is Editor of *TriQuarterly* magazine and Co-founder and Co-editor of TriQuarterly Books.

MATT HART's poetry can be heard, most recently, on the CD, "This Is Our Music," from the art-rock band Travel (Deary Me Records, 2000). His poems have appeared in *Conduit, River City, Spinning Jenny*, and *Swerve*. He co-founded and co-edits *Forklift, Ohio: A Journal of Poetry, Cooking & Light Industrial Safety*.

KRISTEN HAVENS is a New England native and aspiring sitcom writer. Her poetry, fiction and essays have appeared in *Renaissance Magazine*,

Poems *Niederngassne*, *3rd Muse*, and the *New England Intercollegiate Library Journal*. She was a semifinalist in the 2000 Chesterfield Film Company/Writers Film Project competition.

GEORGE HIGGINS is an Assistant Public Defender in Alameda County, California. He graduated from the University of Michigan Law School, and is an MFA candidate at Warren Wilson College. His work has been published in *Squaw Review*, with poems forthcoming in *Pleiades*.

TONY HOAGLAND is getting close to having a third collection of poems. His second collection, *Donkey Gospel*, was published by Graywolf Press. He is concerned about the epidemic use of the fragment in contemporary poetry. He teaches at the University of Pittsburgh.

CHRISTINA K. HUTCHINS teaches at the Pacific School of Religion, Berkeley, CA, and is a Ph.D. candidate in Interdisciplinary Studies at the Graduate Theological Union in Berkeley. Recent poems appear in *Cream City Review*, *Nimrod*, *Calyx*, *Fireweed*, *Thema*, *Iris*, *Portland Review*, *Southern Poetry Review*, *Bay Windows*, *Paterson Literary Review*, *Harvard Gay and Lesbian Review*, *Journal of Women and Religion*, *Talking River Review*, *Paideusis: Journal of Interdisciplinary and Cross-Cultural Studies*, and in various anthologies. She has won the International Haiku Society's Senryu Award, the Villa Montalvo Poetry Prize, and a Barbara Deming/Memorial Fund for Women Poetry Award.

MARK IRWIN is the author of four books of poetry, most recently *White City* which was nominated for the National Book Critics Circle Award and received the Colorado Book Award.

ROY JACOBSTEIN's *Blue Numbers, Red Life* won the 2000 Harperprints Chapbook Competition. He also received *Mid-America Review's* James Wright Prize. Recent work has appeared in a number of literary venues, including *Witness*, *Threepenny Review*, *Quarterly West*, *Prairie Schooner*, *Poetry Northwest*, and *Parnassus*. A former official of the U.S. Agency for International Development, he works as an international public health physician and lives in Chapel Hill, NC.

KATE KNAPP JOHNSON is the author of three collections of poetry: *When Orchids Were Flowers* (Dragon Gate, Inc.), *This Perfect Life* (Miami University Press) and, her recently published *Wind Somewhere, and Shade* (Miami University Press, 2001). She teaches in the graduate and undergraduate writing programs at Sarah Lawrence College and is a student at The Westchester Institute for Training in Psychoanalysis. She lives in Somers, NY with her husband and children.

KAREN KEVORKIAN has published poetry and fiction in *Fiction International, Massachusetts Review, Virginia Quarterly Review, Antioch Review, Third Coast, Five Fingers Review*, and *Hambone*. She has twice won *Mississippi Review* fiction awards, and has held residencies at MacDowell and Djerassi. She works in San Francisco as an editor of exhibition catalogues for an art museum.

SUSAN KOLODNY'S poems appear in *New England Review, River Styx, Green Mountains Review, ThreePenny Review*, and in recent anthologies. She is the author of a book of prose nonfiction, *The Captive Muse: On Cretaivity and Its Inhibition* (PsychoSocial Press, 2000).

RICHARD KOSTELANETZ has individual entries appearing in *Contemporary Poets, Contemporary Novelists, Postmodern Fiction, Baker's Biographical Dictionary of Musicians, A Reader's Guide to Twentieth-Century Writers*, the *Mirriam-Webster Encyclopedia of Literature, Webster's Dictionary of American Authors*, and *Britannica.com*, among other selective directories. Living in New York, where he was born, he still needs $1.50 (US) to take a subway.

PETER LEVITT is a poet and translator who received a Lannan Foundation Literary Award in Poetry. His contribution this issue will be included in his book whose working title is *Writing Spirit*, due out from Harmony Books in January 2003.

GARY LILLEY, born and raised in Sandy Cross, North Carolina, resides in Washington, D.C. He has received the DC Commission of the Arts Fellowship for Poetry in 2000 and 1996, and is presently a student in Warren Wilson College's MFA Program.

GERALD LOCKLIN has published over eighty books and chapbooks of petry and fiction. He has won numerous awards in both poetry and prose, including the Pushcart Prize. He currently resides in Long Beach, California, where he teaches Creative Writing and Literature at California State University, Long Beach.

JEFFREY McDANIEL is the author of *Alibi* and *The Forgiveness Parade*, both published by Manic D Press. His poems have appeared in many literary magazines and anthologies, including *Best American Poetry 1994, New (American) Poets, The New Young American Poets, American Poetry: The Next Generation*, and *Ploughshares*.

FRED MORAMARCO is Editor of *Poetry International*, a poetry annual published at San Diego State University where he teaches American

Literature and Creative Writing. He is co-author of *Containing Multitudes: Poetry in the United States Since 1950* and *Modern American Poetry*, and co-editor of *Men of Our Time: Male Poetry in Contemporary America*.

CHRISTOPHER MOYLAN's poetry and prose poems have appeared in many journals, including *The Prose Poem Review*, *Negative Capability*, *Furious Fictions*, *The Widener Review*, *Proteus*, and the Italian journals *Trame* and *Tempo Presente*.

ELISABETH MURAWSKI's book, *Moon and Mercury*, was published in 1990 by Washington Writers' Publishing House. Her chapbook, *Troubled by an Angel*, was published by Cleveland State University Poetry Center in 1997. Her poems have appeared in numerous journals and magazines, including *Hayden's Ferry Review*, *The New Republic*, *Grand Street*, *American Poetry Review*, *Virginia Quarterly Review*, *Shenandoah*, and *Quarterly West*.

MURIEL NELSON is a graduate of the Warren Wilson Program for Writers. A poem from her book *Part Song* (Bear Star Press, 1999) was nominated for a Pushcart Prize. Other poems have been published or are forthcoming in *The New Republic*, *Ploughshares*, *Marlboro Review*, *Northwest Review*, *The Christian Century*, *The Prague Post*, and *Heliotrope*.

D. NURKSE's fifth collection *Leaving Xaia* was published by Four Way Books in 2000. New work includes *The Rules of Paradise* (Four Way Books, 2001), *The Fall* (Knopf, forthcoming), and poems in *The New Yorker* and *The Paris Review*.

LOUIS PHILLIPS is a poet, playwright, and short-story writer. SMU Press published his collection of stories, *A Dream Where No One Dare Lives*, and Fort Schuyler Press will soon publish his new collection of stories, *The Bus to the Moon*. He has published over 35 books for children and adults.

JAMES REISS' fourth collection of poems, *Ten Thousand Good Mornings*, was published by Carnegie Mellon earlier this year. New work is appearing, or soon will appear, in *Free Lunch*, *The Formalist*, *The Nation*, *The Nebraska Review*, and *Slate*.

LEE ROSSI is the author of *Beyond Rescue*. His work has appeared in the anthologies *Grand Passion*, *Truth & Lies That Press for Life*, and *New Los Angeles Poets*, as well as in journals such as *The Sun*, *Poetry East*, *Chelsea*, *The Wormwood Review*, *Poetry/LA* and *The Los Angeles Times*. He has also served as editor of the early 90's poetry magazine *Tsunami* and on the Organizing Committee of the Los Angeles Poetry Festival.

AMANDA SCHAFFER's work has appeared or is forthcoming in *Ploughshares, Colorado Review, Spinning Jenny,* and *Green Mountain Review,* among others. She teaches chemistry in New York City.

BARRY SILESKY is the author of a book of prose poems, *One Thing That Can Save Us* (Coffee House Press, 1992). His prose poems have appeared in many magazines, including *New Directions Annual, Prose Poem, Fiction, Tampa Review, Chelsea,* and the recent University of Iowa Press anthology *American Diaspora.* He edits the journal *ACM,* and teaches at the School of the Art Institute of Chicago.

ANNE SILVER has an M.A. in Poetry and and M.S. in Psychology. Her poems have appeared in numerous journals including *Nimrod, Porcupine, Poem,* and *Bridges.*

RICK SMITH writes (*The Wren Notebook, 2000,* Lummox Press), plays blues harp with The Hangan Brothers (Mars Market, 2000, Bue Cap Music) and co-directs Back in the Saddle, a long term residential program for head injured adults in Apple Valley, California. He is a Clinical Psychologist with a specialty in domestic violence. He lives with his wife and their 7-year-old son.

ADRIENNE SU is the author of the poetry collection *Middle Kingdom* (Alice James, 1997), and is poet-in-residence at Dickinson College in Carlisle, Pennsylvania. Her poems have appeared in *Best American Poetry 2000, The New American Poets: A Bread Loaf Anthology,* and *American Poetry: The Next Generation.*

VIRGIL SUÁREZ was born in Havana, Cuba in 1962. Since 1974 he has lived in the United States. He is the author of four novels, a collection of stories. His memoirs *Spared Angola: Memories of a Cuban-American Childhood* and *Café Nostalgia* chronicle his life of exile in both Cuba and the United States. His the author of four collections of poetry: *Garabato Poems, You Come Singing, In the Republic of Longing,* and *Palm Crows,* forthcoming this year from the University of Arizona Press in its "Camino del Sol" series.

ELAINE TERRANOVA is the author of three books of poems: *The Cult of the Right Hand,* winner of the 1990 Walt Whitman Award; *Damages*; and *The Dog's Heart,* forthcoming from Orchises Press. Her verse translation of Euripides' *Iphigenia at Aulis,* is part of the Penn Greek Drama Series. Her poems have appeared in *Prairie Schooner, The New Yorker, The American Poetry Review, Boulevard* and other magazines. She was awarded an NEA fellowship in literature in 1997.

DAVID TRINIDAD's latest book of poems, *Plasticville*, was published by Turtle Point Press in 2000. His other books include *Answer Song* (High Risk Books, 1994), *Hand Over Heart 1981-1988* (Amethyst Press, 1991), and *Pavane* (Sherwood Press, 1981). He teaches poetry at Rutgers University, where he directs the Writers at Rutgers series, and is a member of the core faculty in the MFA writing program at The New School.

WILLIAM TROWBRIDGE is the author of the books *Flickers, O Paradise, Enter Dark Stranger* (University of Arkansas Press, 2000, 1995, 1989), and *The Book of Kong* (chapbook, Iowa State University Press, 1986). His poems have appeared or are forthcoming in *The Gettysburg Review, Poetry, The Georgia Review, Crazyhorse, Boulevard, The Southern Review, Prairie Schooner, Epoch, New Letters*, and many others. He is an associate editor of *The Laurel Review*.

LEE UPTON's fourth book of poetry, *Civilian Histories*, appeared in 2000 from the University of Georgia Press. Her third book of literary criticism, *The Muse of Abandonment*, was published by Bucknell University Press.

AMY UYEMATSU is a teacher and poet from Los Angeles. She is sansei, third-generation Japanese American. Her second book, *Nights of Fire, Nights of Rain*, (Story Line Press, 1998), is currently available.

DAVID WAGONER has published sixteen books of poems, most recently *Traveling Light: Collected and New Poems* (University of Illinois Press, 1999), winner of the William Stafford Memorial Award given by Pacific Northwest Booksellers, and ten novels, one of which, *The Escape Artist*, was made into a movie by Francis Ford Coppola. He won the Lilly Prize in 1991, has been nominated twice for the National Book Award, and has won the Zabel Prize, the Blumenthal-Leviton-Blonder Prize, the Eunice Tietjens Prize, the English-speaking Union Prize, the Levinson Prize, and the Union League Prize of POETRY (Chicago). He was a chancellor of the Academy of American Poets for 23 years. He has taught at the University of Washington since 1954 and is the editor of *Poetry Northwest*. The University of Illinois Press will publish his book *The House of Song* in 2002.

JESSE WATERS currently heads the Graduate Creative Writing Association at The University of North Carolina at Wilmington's MFA program. His work has appeared in *Atlantis, Plainsongs,* and *Cimarron Review*. He is the Managing Editor of *Slide*.

CHARLES HARPER WEBB's latest collection of poems, *Liver*, won the 1999 Felix Pollak Prize and was published by the University of Wisconsin

Press. A new collection, *Tulip Farms and Liver Colonies*, will be published this fall by BOA Editions. He teaches at California State University, Long Beach, and is a 2001-2002 Guggenheim fellow.

ROGER WEINGARTEN's eight collections of poems include *Ghost Wrestling*, *Infant Bonds of Joy*, and *Shadow Shadow*, all from David R. Godine; his anthologies include *New American Poets of the '90s*, *Ghost Writing: Haunted Tales by Contemporary Writers*, *Poets of the New Century*, and *Manthology: Poems of the Male Experience* forthcoming from Invisible Cities Press next fall. He edits the Invisible Cities Press poetry series. He founded and teaches in the MFA in Writing at Vermont College of The Union Institute, where he also teaches in and directs the Post-Graduate Writers' Conference. His awards include a National Endowment for the Arts Fellowship and an Ingram Merrill Award in Literature.

KATHLEENE K. WEST has published nine books of poery and fiction including *The Farmer's Daughter*, *Water Witching*, *Death of a Regional Poet*, and the bi-lingual *Romance Tercermundista/Third World Romance*, published in Cuba. She is the poetry editor of *Puerto del Sol*.

EVE WOOD is a writer and artist living in Los Angeles. Her poems have appeared in many journals, including *Best American Poetry 1997*, *The New Republic*, *TriQuarterly*, *The Seattle Review*, *Poetry*, and *The Antioch Review*. Her chapbook *Paper Frankenstein* waas published by Beyond Baroque in 1998, and her book *Correspondences* was published in Europe in 1999.

GAIL WRONSKY is the author of two books of poetry, *Dying for Beauty* and *Again the Gemini Are in the Orchard*. Her poems and critical essays have appeared in *Antioch Review*, *Denver Quarterly*, *Colorado Review*, *Boston Review*, *Virginia Quarterly Review* and other journals. She is the recipient of an Artists Fellowship from the California Arts Council. Her first novel, *The Love-talkers*, was recently published by Hollyridge Press.

DEAN YOUNG's new book, Skid, will be out from University of Pittsburgh Press in the spring.

"There's hopped-up frenzy and plenty of wit here."
— **Kirkus Reviews**

JACK KEROUAC'S AVATAR ANGEL
His Last Novel
by CHUCK ROSENTHAL

ISBN 0-9676003-2-4
$23.95 Hardcover

Chuck Rosenthal discovers a lost, unpublished manuscript from the King of the Beats—Jack Kerouac—who returns from the grave to set off one last time, charting chart the experience and conscience of a generation grappling with a changed culture. At once visionary and elegant, restless and incantatory, Rosenthal's writing achieves a rare beauty, his sensitivity to language as great as Kerouac's. In an exuberant novel of great wit and great loss, the emptiness Kerouac encounters in this final journey is palpable and tragic, unforeseen but inevitable, both familiar and foreign to America's most famous mystic traveler.

"You will be dazzled and amazed."
— David St. John

THE LOVE-TALKERS
An Erotic Fable
by GAIL WRONSKY

ISBN 0-9676003-3-2
$23.95 Hardcover

The beauty of Gail Wronsky's poetic language has never been better displayed than in *The Love-talkers*. Mexico City, with its parks and cathedrals provides a lush backdrop for the story. A sumptuously rendered book, celebrating passionate imagination with all the sublime joy of physical love, Wronsky's elegiac style summons up the magic of Latin American fiction in this novel of desire which brings us into the depths of erotic charge. From ecstatic awakenings to feverish enactments of appetite, Wronsky's novel reveals what happens when we find our deepest yearnings made true.

"An amazing use of language and clarity of description compels the reader on."
—**Patricia Gulian**, *Book/Mark*

HUNGER
and Other Stories
by Ian Randall Wilson

ISBN 0-9676003-0-8
$12.95 Paperback

In his first collection of short stories, Ian Randall Wilson's characters are driven by intense yearnings for the satisfaction of their most basic human desires. All are thwarted by personal shortcomings, or the shortcomings of others, in their attempts to fulfill their longing. Here are 14 stories which "despite their restlessness," former *North American Review* editor Robley Wilson says, "glitter with persistent hopes."

"Alexander is an accomplished writer with a deft hand for characterization."
— **Hillary Johnson**, *LA Weekly*

THE FINAL AUDIT
and Other Stories
by Ronald Alexander

ISBN 0-9676003-1-6
$12.95 Paperback

In Ronald Alexander's debut novel, Dexter Giles lives a double life, balancing a straight-jacketed career in the homophobic towers of corporate culture with his secret world as a gay man. Nancy Lamb writes, "The interconnected stories in this novel are serious and unforgettable and told with humor and insight. Alexander displays an intuitive grasp of the complexity of family relationships and the power of long-term friendships."

Guidelines

✂ cut along dotted lines

Submission Guidelines

Unless accompanied by an original proof-of-purchase, unsolicited submissions will be considered March 1 through May 31 only. Unsolicited submissions postmarked outside that window will be returned unread. Submissions accompanied by an original proof-of-purchase will be considered year round.

Manuscripts must be limited to five poems per submission with author name and address appearing on each page. Long poems not exceeding ten single spaced typewritten pages will be considered, but poems longer than three pages must be submitted separately.

Essays and reviews will also be considered. Please limit essays to no more than ten pages, double-spaced. Reviews must be no more than eight double-spaced pages.

Include a self-addressed, stamped envelope for return of manuscripts. Submissions without SASE will be discarded unread. No cover letter is necessary. No simultaneous submissions or previously published material will be considered. We report on submissions within one to three months. Manuscripts accepted after May 31 will appear the following calendar year.

Mail submissions to: Editor, 88, c/o Hollyridge Press, P. O. Box 2872, Venice, CA 90294

Guidelines

✂ cut along dotted lines

Submission Guidelines

Unless accompanied by an original proof-of-purchase, unsolicited submissions will be considered March 1 through May 31 only. Unsolicited submissions postmarked outside that window will be returned unread. Submissions accompanied by an original proof-of-purchase will be considered year round.

Manuscripts must be limited to five poems per submission with author name and address appearing on each page. Long poems not exceeding ten single spaced typewritten pages will be considered, but poems longer than three pages must be submitted separately.

Essays and reviews will also be considered. Please limit essays to no more than ten pages, double-spaced. Reviews must be no more than eight double-spaced pages.

Include a self-addressed, stamped envelope for return of manuscripts. Submissions without SASE will be discarded unread. No cover letter is necessary. No simultaneous submissions or previously published material will be considered. We report on submissions within one to three months. Manuscripts accepted after May 31 will appear the following calendar year.

Mail submissions to: Editor, 88, c/o Hollyridge Press, P. O. Box 2872, Venice, CA 90294